THE POLYMATH'S PATH

THE POLYMATH'S PATH

I WANT TO LEARN EVERYTHING:
THE POLYMATH'S PATH

By Gabriel P. Elbert-Rasmussen

I Want To Learn Everything: The Polymath's Path

ISBN   *979-8-9936543-1-7 Paperback*
        979-8-9936543-0-0 Hardcover
        979-8-9936543-2-4 Ebook

Table of Content

I Want to Learn Everything

The Polymath's Path

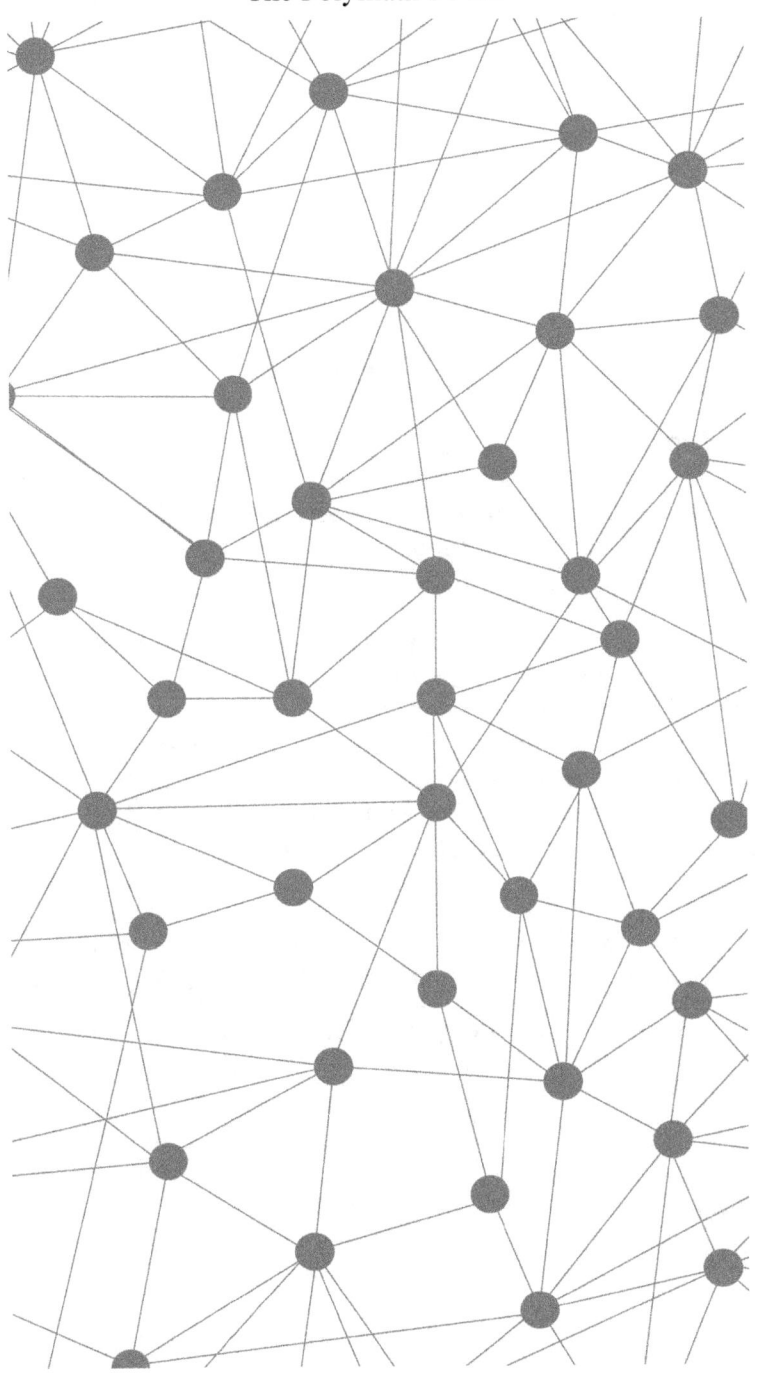

Foreword

I've never written a book before, and I am still growing and learning about how I think and learn. However, I know enough to share my experiences and understandings of what I've discovered along the way.

Thanks to my parents, who carried a wide breadth of knowledge and ingrained that love of learning into my siblings and me; to my sisters, who have always given me new perspectives and ideas, and let me bounce my thoughts against theirs; to my teachers, who inspired curiosity; and to all the books, conversations, and films that left their mark on me.

This book is not a final word on polymathy. It is a guide, an invitation, and a companion for those who feel called to

learn broadly, deeply, and with joy.

The Polymath's Path

*For every curious mind who ever wanted to learn every-
thing — may this book inspire you.*

Dedication

This book is dedicated to my loving family, whose constant support has shaped every part of my journey.
To my parents, who have guided and encouraged me through all my interests.
To my godmother, who first sparked my curiosity about understanding my own way of thinking.
To my sisters, who teach me new things each day and give me the joy of being a guide in return.
To my bedsteforældre (grandparents) and Nana, whose patience and care have been a steady presence through-out my life.
And to all my friends, who help me grow beyond what I ever thought possible.

I love you all deeply, and I thank you profusely.

A Note on Perspective

This book cannot be perfect for everyone. The hope is that it will be greatly helpful, but I write with my own background, strengths, and limitations.

I am a white, straight, man who grew up in the Chicano- and Latino-influenced area of San Diego, California. I am Danish-American, with Irish, German, French, Southern, Midwestern, and Southwestern cultural roots. My family is primarily agricultural. I have ADHD, I am a social introvert, and I have been fortunate to grow up with a supportive family and strong friend groups.

These perspectives inevitably shape how I see the world, and how I present learning and polymathy. They may not reflect the experiences of everyone who reads this book. My goal is not to speak for every background, but to offer my own process, with the hope that you can adapt it to

your own life.

Introduction

When I was a kid, my parents always had something going on: making cheese, fixing plumbing, fermenting hard cider, gardening, speaking at conferences, cooking, drawing, studying maps, learning mythology, or debating politics. They ran businesses, spoke multiple languages, and pursued knowledge with curiosity and courage.

Needless to say, their autodidactic approach to life rubbed off on me. Every interest I had — from dinosaurs and chemistry, to theatre and cooking — was encouraged and guided. By the time I was in high school, I had explored bushcraft, astronomy, languages, fitness, and countless creative pursuits.

*But it wasn't until later that I learned there was a word for this way of life: **polymath.** A person who seeks breadth and depth across multiple domains, weaving them together into insight and practice. Discovering that word gave me clarity — not just for what I was, but for what I could become.*

The purpose of this book is not to make you a master of everything. It is to give you the tools, mindsets, and starting points to live like a polymath: curious, creative,

humble, and connected.

Preface

I Want to Learn Everything: The Polymath's Path is a book that takes interdisciplinary learning and strips it down to its brass tacks.

For me, the idea of being a "polymath" or "Renaissance person" simply sounded cool at first. But over time, I found that the ability to draw from many different fields—and to live within them simultaneously—became easier, richer, and more natural.

This book was made for everyone. If you can read or listen to it, it's for you. I've focused on the systems and habits that shape polymathic thinking, removing references to any one profession or specialty. That way, you can apply its lessons to your own personal and professional life—and if you share it with someone else, they can do the same through their own lens. It's meant to be a book for everyone, from every path.

Whether you are a professional seeking to grow in your career and become a resource for others, a business leader wanting to strengthen your team's adaptability, a parent hoping to nurture your child's curiosity and possibilities, or simply an individual eager to understand the world more freely—this book will help you find your way forward.

As you begin, take a moment to pause and reflect on who you are and what truly interests you—whether that be growth, curiosity, or mastery. Then, as you read, treat these pages not as a list of answers, but as a guide.

This book was written for you, and only you can learn what you need from it.

How to read this book

This book was written to be both a guide and a companion. You don't need to read it cover to cover in order. But a few chapters form the foundations for everything that follows.

Start with:
Chapter 1 — What Is a Polymath?
This chapter defines the word itself and introduces the mindset behind it. It's where you'll discover what it truly means to think and live like a polymath.

Chapter 2 — The Forest of the Mind
This is the metaphorical framework for the entire book — a map of how your interests grow, connect, and evolve. Once you understand your "forest," everything else in the book becomes easier to apply.

After that, you can **explore Section One** in any order.

Section One, *The Polymath's Toolkit,* is about *systems*

how to think, learn, and grow across fields. Each chapter is a standalone tool you can apply right away. You might choose to read the chapters that resonate most with your current goals, whether that's discussion, note-taking, or reframing your mindset.

Section Two, *The Disciplines*, is about *practice*

It's a field guide to getting started — you can jump directly to the discipline that interests you most. Each one includes a short introduction, a practical first step, and a "Skills" list to help you align that subject in your own life.

You can read this book straight through or wander freely — like walking through your own forest of learning. The only rule is curiosity.

SECTION ONE: The Polymath's Toolkit

How to think, learn, and grow like a polymath.

Section One Foreword:

Before diving into specific fields of knowledge, we need to prepare the mind. This section is about the habits, tools, and perspectives that make polymathy possible.

Here, we'll look at how to build your forest of learning, how to reframe curiosity as abundance, how to use hobbies as entry points, and how to develop practices like discussion, teaching, note-keeping, and readiness.

Think of this as your foundation. You don't need to master it all before moving on, but the ideas here will give you confidence and clarity — the compass and tools you'll carry into the rest of your journey.

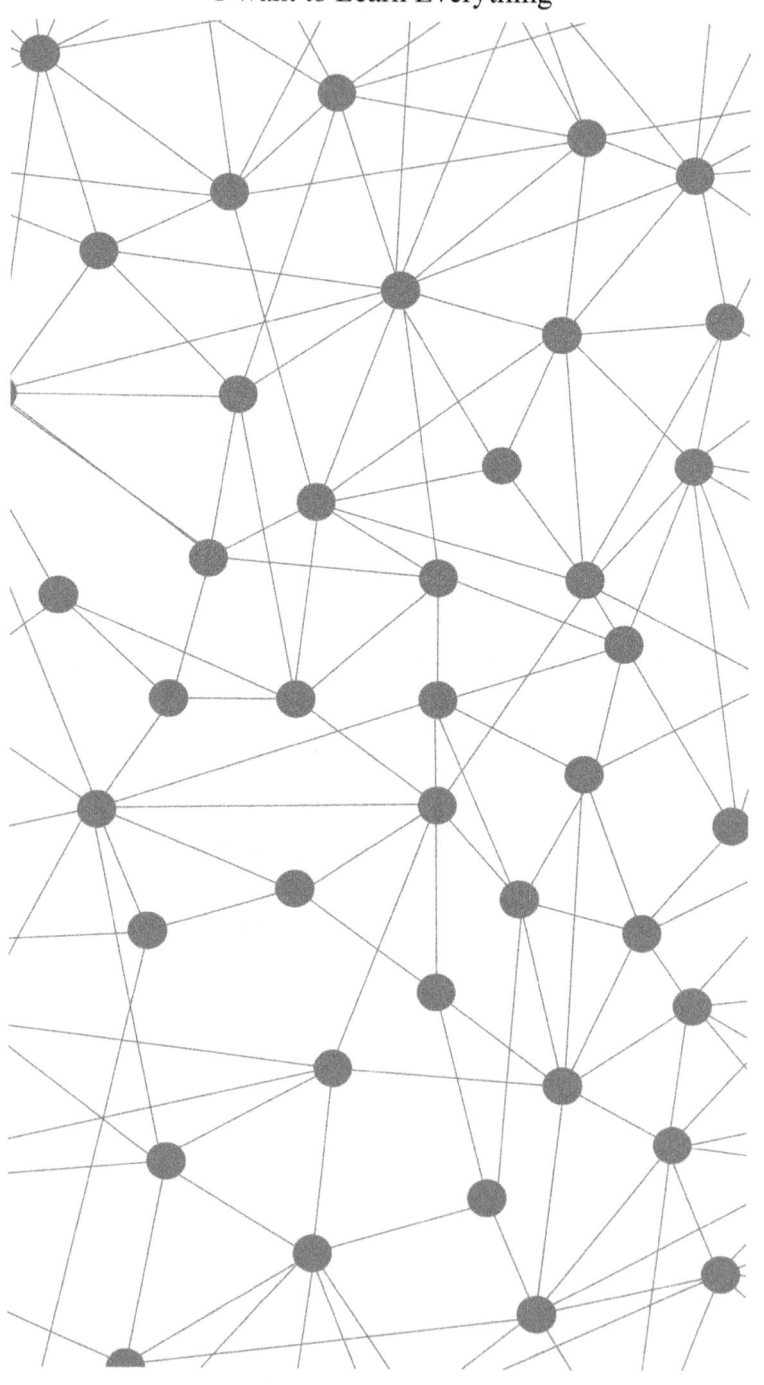

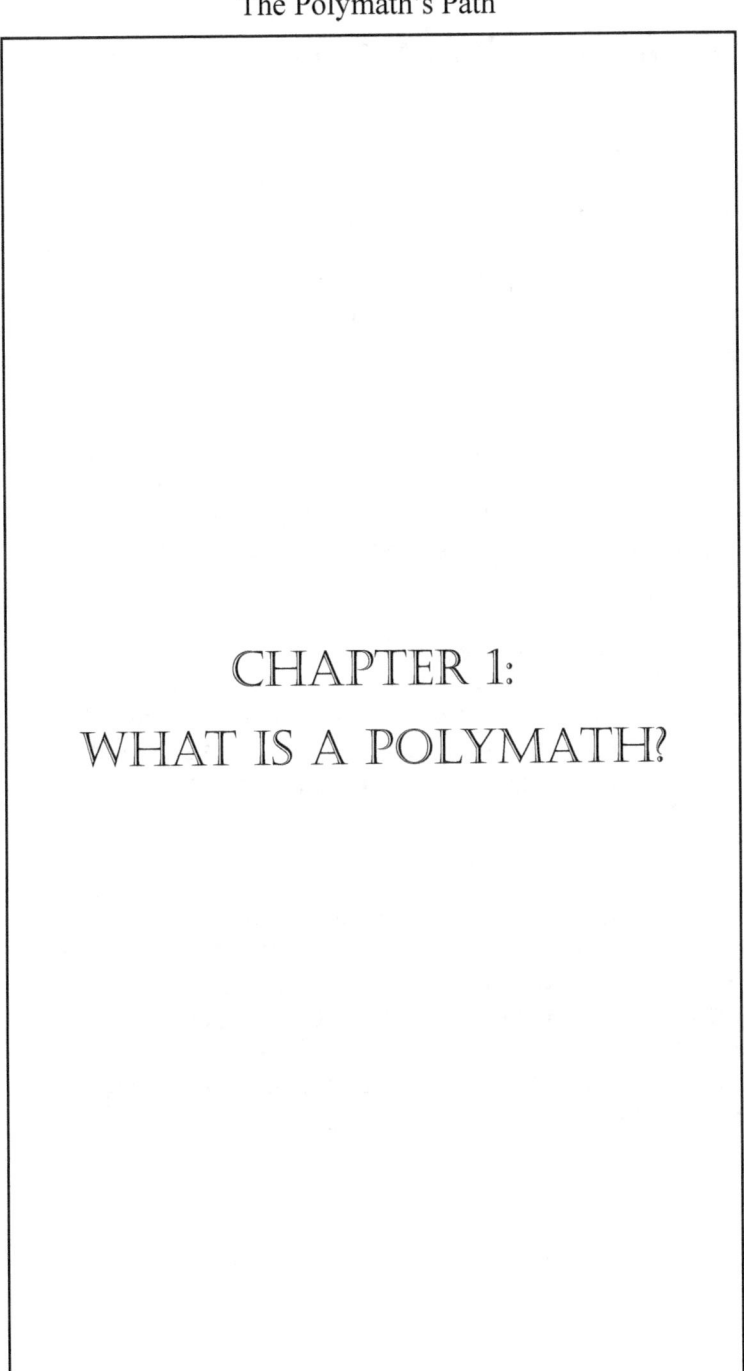

CHAPTER 1:
WHAT IS A POLYMATH?

What Is a Polymath?

Definitions:
The word *polymath* is familiar to many, but few know its full etymology. It comes from the Greek: *polu-* meaning "many" or "much," and *manthanein*, meaning "to learn" or "to study." Combined, they formed *polumathēs*—"having learned much"—which evolved into *polymath* in the early 17th century.

An alternate term, *polyhistor*, shares similar roots: *polu-* ("many") and *histor* ("wise man" or "learned one"). This evolved into *poluhistor*—"very learned"—and entered English usage in the late 16th century.

The Essence of a Polymath:
A polymath is someone who pursues *both breadth and depth* of knowledge across multiple domains. They don't just dabble—they seek mastery in several fields and connect insights across them to generate new ideas and solve complex problems.

In my view, a person qualifies as a polymath with deep knowledge in at least **three distinct areas**. For a more technical comparison, consider the term *polyglot*, which typically refers to someone who speaks **four or more languages** fluently. A polymath, likewise, blends mastery across multiple fields—three to four being a practical starting point.

Generalist – The Horizontal Thinker

A **generalist** has wide-ranging knowledge across many domains but may not possess deep expertise in each. They're excellent at connecting ideas, adapting quickly, and managing diverse challenges.

Examples:

- **Contractors** – understand multiple trades and coordinate specialists.
- **Project Managers** – guide complex systems without being experts in every task.
- **General Practitioners** – have a broad view of medicine and refer to specialists when needed.
- **Educators (especially K–8)** – teach multiple subjects and foster integrated thinking.

Analogy: Generalists think **horizontally**—they see the full landscape.

Specialist – The Vertical Thinker

A **specialist** focuses deeply on a single topic or niche. They often drive innovation or precision in their field, though sometimes at the expense of flexibility.

Examples:

- **Neurosurgeons** – highly trained in a narrow but life-critical domain.

- **Ph.D. Researchers** – often spend years refining a specific theory or mechanism.

- **Watchmakers** – master the micro-mechanics of precision timekeeping.

- **Lawyers (e.g., tax or patent law)** – navigate narrow but highly complex legal fields.

Analogy: Specialists think **vertically**—they dig deep.

"A polymath is someone who pursues both breadth and depth of knowledge..."

Polymath – The Web Builder

A **polymath** blends the generalist's range with the specialist's rigor. They may not cover as many fields as a generalist or reach the extreme heights of a specialist in one area—but the combination of moderate-to-deep mastery across several fields makes them uniquely equipped to synthesize and innovate ideas into new systems and solutions that none of the individual fields could reach alone.

Historical Examples:

- **Leonardo da Vinci** – Artist, engineer, anatomist, and inventor.

- **Benjamin Franklin** – Statesman, scientist, printer, inventor, and philosopher.

- **Maya Angelou** – Poet, dancer, filmmaker, activist,

- actress, and memoirist.

- **Alexander von Humboldt** – Geographer, naturalist, botanist, climatologist, explorer, and philosopher.

- **Ada Lovelace** – Mathematician, visionary, and the world's first computer programmer.

Modern Examples:

- **Neri Oxman** – Architect, biologist, materials scientist, engineer, and designer.

- **Neil deGrasse Tyson** – Astrophysicist, communicator, educator, and public policy advisor.

- **Natalie Portman** – Actress, neuroscientist, director, activist, and writer.

- **Donald Glover (Childish Gambino)** – Musician, actor, director, writer, and comedian.

- **Mae Jemison** – Astronaut, medical doctor, engineer, dancer, educator, and even a Star Trek guest star.

Analogy: Polymaths think **horizontally, vertically, and diagonally**. They build *webs*—connecting unexpected nodes across disciplines to reveal new patterns.

The Specialist–Generalist Wave

Throughout history, the world has swung like a tide between two priorities: specialization and generalization. During one era, specialists lead — diving deep into narrow fields to perfect new tools, technologies, or ideas. Then, as innovation stagnates from over-focus, generalists rise — weaving disciplines together, translating discoveries, and opening new frontiers.

23

This rhythm — expansion and contraction, deepening and broadening — forms what I call the Specialist–Generalist Wave. Picture a sine wave rolling through time. At one peak, precision dominates; at the next, synthesis does. But running between both curves is a steady current: the polymath.

The polymath doesn't wait for the wave to shift — they surf it. They learn deeply enough to contribute, broadly enough to connect, and rhythmically enough to stay relevant across changing tides. Understanding this cycle helps you see that your curiosity is not a distraction — it's evolution's rhythm calling you forward.

The Specialist–Generalist Wave

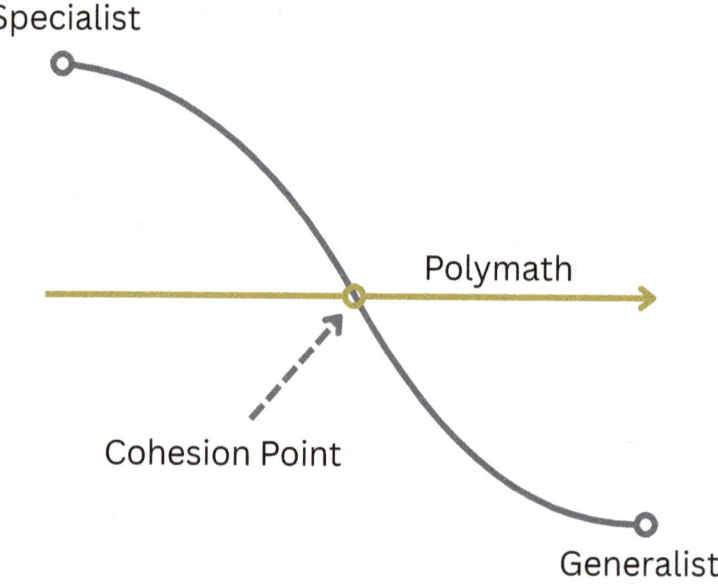

Specialist

Polymath

Cohesion Point

Generalist

Your effect as a polymath

To be a polymath is to live curiously — but also to use that curiosity to serve. Every person you meet. every system you touch, benefits when you draw connections others can't yet see. Whether you're designing better tools and systems, teaching with empathy, creating art that sparks dialogue, or simply listening with broader understanding, you turn knowledge into nourishment. A productive polymath doesn't just collect information; they cultivate it for others.

Value to the Individual
For the individual, polymathy brings vitality — a life that never stops unfolding. It trains flexibility of mind, a deeper sense of purpose, and the joy of connecting what others keep separate. It gives you a language for your curiosity and the confidence to keep learning long after formal education ends.

Value to the Community
In community, polymaths become connectors. They translate between specialists, bridge cultural gaps, and turn shared curiosity into collaboration. Their breadth of interest makes them natural teachers and listeners — people who weave networks rather than walls.

and finally —

Value to the Society
For society, polymaths are catalysts of renewal. The world's great challenges rarely fit within one discipline, and the polymath's ability to combine science, art, and ethics gives rise to new solutions — and new beauty. They remind us that progress depends not only on depth, but depth *with* connection.

Polymath Prompt

Think of one subject you know well, one subject you dabble in, and one subject you've always wanted to explore.

How might these three connect?

The Polymath's Path

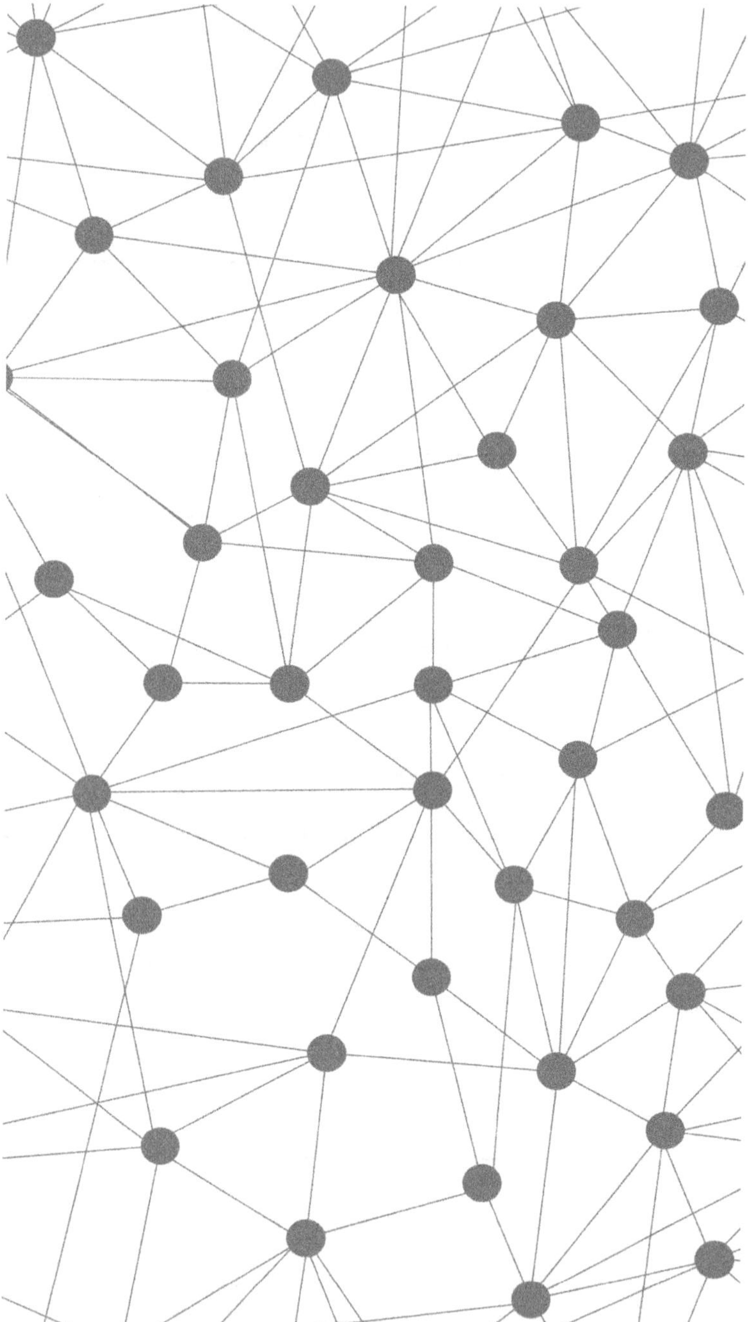

CHAPTER 2:
THE FOREST OF THE MIND

The Forest of the Mind

Cultivating Depth in a Sea of Curiosity

The primary issue with beginning a study into polymathy is becoming overwhelmed. The world is vast, overflowing with knowledge, skills, and experiences. When you first set out to learn "everything," the sheer scale can feel daunting — almost paralyzing.

What I've found most useful is not trying to pursue every subject at once, but noticing the **seeds and saplings** already in your life. These small curiosities and recurring interests, with care, can grow into trees — strong, rooted, and fruitful. Together, they form the beginnings of a **forest of knowledge.**

Choosing 3–5 Core Trees of Interest

You already know your trees, even if you haven't named them yet. They're the interests that keep resurfacing in your life — the hobbies you never quite let go of, the subjects you always perk up for in conversation, the skills you find yourself wanting to refine.

A polymath doesn't need to cultivate an endless forest all at once. Instead, they tend to **a handful of strong trees** that anchor their learning.

I recommend beginning with three. Like the three trunks of a young grove, this creates stability without overwhelming you. Later, you can grow to four or five, and beyond.

Think of the polyglot: someone who speaks four or more

languages fluently. They don't speak every language, but their depth across several makes them able to navigate the world in extraordinary ways. Likewise, the polymath anchors in a few trees, then lets their forest grow outward from there.

A Case Study: Jordan's Forest

Take Jordan. At first glance, Jordan's interests look scattered:

- They love learning languages and practicing conversation.

- They enjoy trying new foods and exploring cultural cuisines.

- They're also a devoted Star Trek fan, fascinated by planetary systems and inter-species relations.

On their own, these may look like three unconnected sprouts. But given time, the saplings start to grow, and the roots begin to entwine.

- **Language** becomes a tree of communication, reaching out like branches to connect people.

- **Food** becomes a tree of cultural connection, rooted in flavor, ritual, and community.

- **Imaginative science fiction** becomes a tree of empathy, teaching Jordan to think about diversity and shared space across boundaries.

Together, these form not just trees, but a **forest of hospitality.**

One day, Jordan might host a dinner party where guests speak to one another in multiple languages, taste new dishes, and discuss stories of imagined cultures. What looks on the surface like three hobbies has become a cultivated domain: the art of welcoming and connecting across difference.

For some this may stay personal — hosting dinners, connecting friends through culture and food. For others, it could become a profession: teaching, hospitality, or intercultural work. The shape doesnt matter as much as the spirit — using curiosity to bring people together.

That's how a polymath grows their forest.

"...tend to a handful of strong trees..."

Roots, Trunks, and Branches

Think of your learning like a tree:

- **Roots** spread wide beneath the surface. They connect with other roots and draw nourishment from many directions. This is the breadth of your curiosity.

- **The trunk** grows tall and steady. This is depth — the steady work of developing mastery in a subject.

- **Branches** reach outward. Each branch is a skill that grows from the trunk. Some sprout further, some wither, and some may even break off and root themselves as new trees.

Over time, your scattered sprouts and branches form not just trees, but a **forest** — an ecosystem of learning that sustains itself.

The Hidden Work of Roots

Growth rarely looks like growth. It often looks like stillness. When we begin learning something new, the surface might show nothing—no visible progress, no measurable improvement. But beneath that stillness, our minds are storing energy and forming hidden connections. Like the roots of a young tree, this early work is quiet, patient, and deliberate.

The first ideas we plant send out fine, hair-like threads into the soil of our memory. They search for meaning, for related concepts, for structure. Over time, these threads strengthen, branch, and find each other underground. Then, seemingly all at once, they burst into new understanding—an "aha" moment that feels sudden but is really the product of weeks or months of invisible effort.

Learning, like nature, follows exponential growth. One connection becomes two, two become four, and before long a web of understanding forms that can hold far more than the sum of its parts. It's the same principle behind the "grains of rice on a chessboard" parable: one step at a time, small additions lead to enormous change.

Even the structure of the brain mirrors this truth. Our dendrites—the branching ends of neurons—spread like the roots of trees, connecting to others and strengthening through repetition. Each new connection is a root that makes the forest of our mind stronger, deeper, and more alive.

A Mental Model of How Ideas Interconnect

The "Forest of the Mind" isn't just a metaphor — it's a framework for visualizing how learning grows. Every curiosity begins as a seed, every effort as a root extending into new soil. Some roots find rich ground, while others wither or rest until conditions change. Over time, these roots feed trunks of deeper mastery, and those trunks branch into skills that reach toward light and connection.

The beauty of this model is that no part stands alone. Roots of one tree feed another; branches cross-pollinate; fallen leaves nourish the soil for new growth. This is how ideas form networks — seemingly unrelated subjects begin to feed one another until knowledge becomes a living ecosystem.

When you learn this way, you stop chasing isolated subjects and start tending a garden of relationships. You can feel when one idea strengthens another, or when a neglected curiosity quietly calls for attention like an unwatered sapling.

My Own Forest (So Far)

When I look at my own life, I see four trees that have grown strong:

- **Performance** – I've been an actor since age four, and performance continues to shape how I think, move, and express.

- **Artisanal Crafts** – My studies in wood-working, herbal medicine, and fermentation anchor me in the art of life.

- **Physical Mastery** – Fitness, water polo, and field-craft train my body as well as my mind.

- **Storytelling, Mythology, & Philosophy** – My lifelong fascination with narrative, wisdom, and meaning forms a foundation that touches everything else I do.

These weren't planted all at once. They grew from scattered seeds — theatre, music, history, and science — into saplings, and then into trees. Now their roots interweave, their branches cross, and together they form the living forest of my learning.

The Generalist, the Specialist, and the Polymath

- A **generalist** spreads roots widely, connecting many subjects. Their value is in making networks and seeing how things relate.

- A **specialist** grows a single trunk tall and strong, reaching for depth and precision. Their value is in focus and mastery.

- A **polymath** cultivates a **forest**: several strong trees, each with roots and branches that interact, connect, and cross-pollinate. Their value is in weaving breadth and depth into a living ecosystem.

- This isn't a hierarchy. Each path has value. The difference is simply how you choose to grow.

Evolving Forests

Your forest doesn't need to be fixed forever. In fact, it will shift.

- A sprout you once ignored may become a tree.
- A branch may break off and root itself as a new

- trunk.

- A tree may wither, but its roots will nourish others.

What matters is that you tend what you have now. The forest will evolve as you do.

Closing Thought
Your interests aren't random. They are seeds. With time and attention, they grow into trees, and the trees connect into forests. This is the polymath's way: not to collect fragments, but to cultivate ecosystems of knowledge.

Polymath Prompt: Tending Your Forest

Look at your own life. Which of your interests are:

- **Seeds** you've only just planted?

- **Branches** of existing trees you're already growing?

- **Saplings** beginning to take shape as full trunks?

How might they connect into a larger forest?

The Polymath's Path

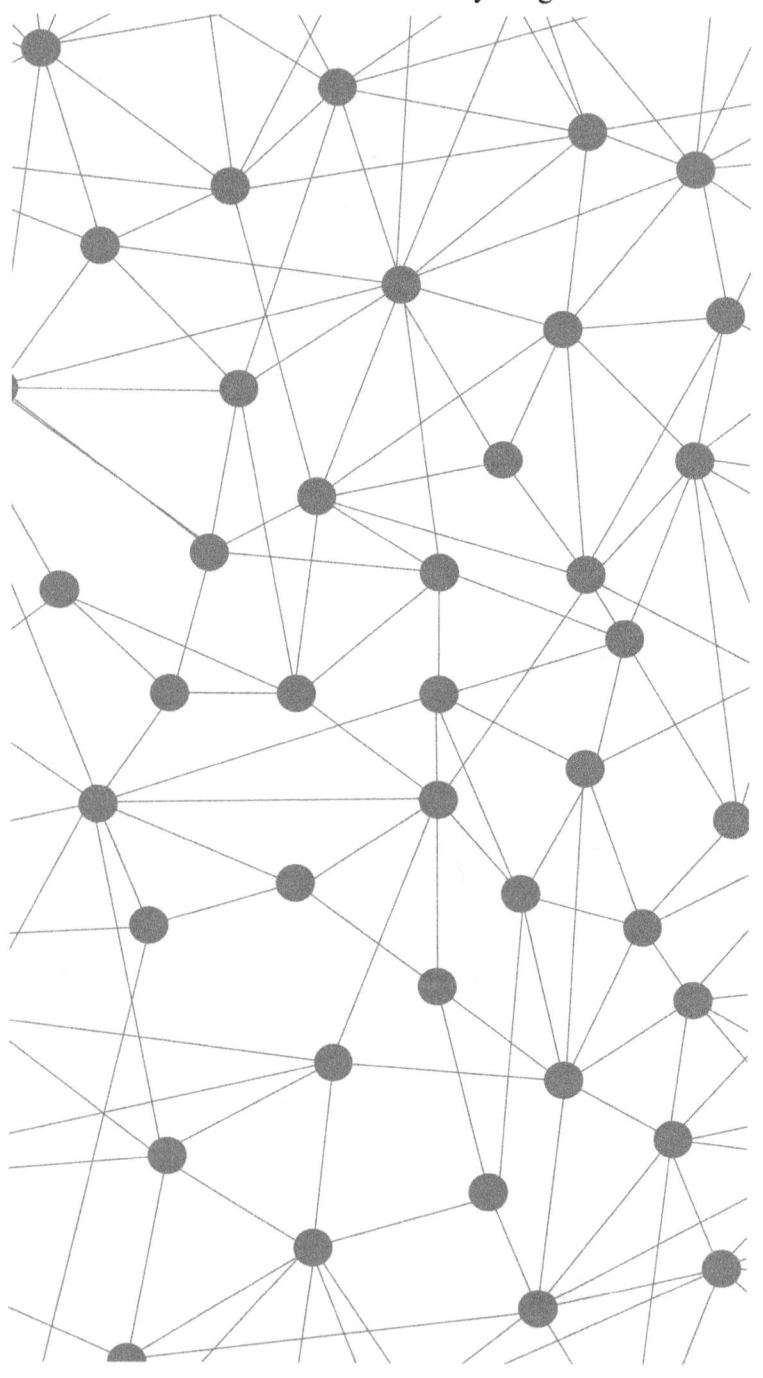

CHAPTER 3:

THE OPTIMIST
VS.
THE PESSIMIST

The Optimist vs. The Pessimist

Reframing Curiosity as Abundance

"Be attentive, do not let the vastness of the world diminish your enthusiasm."

When I began my college studies, I started as a musical theatre major with a woodworking minor. Both were deep interests of mine — by then, I had been acting for 14 years, and my love for traditional and heritage crafts was strong. But as I took those classes, I realized they weren't what I truly wanted for my life. They were wonderful as hobbies, even professions, but not lifestyles for me.

So I became lost. For years I tried to find my path, taking a scattered array of classes in hopes of stumbling upon what I was looking for. Every class fit perfectly into what I now see as my polymathic forest — they grew into trees I still tend today — but at the time, none gave me the sense of a clear life direction. I slipped into a pessimistic mindset, weighed down by the sense that *I had chosen wrong.*

A few years later, I faced a similar situation. I had completed every fermentation class in a fermentation business program, and when I began the business courses associated with the degree, I felt the same dread: *this isn't me.*

But this time, something was different. By then I had embraced polymathy as my framework, and I carried an optimistic mindset. Instead of despairing, I stepped back. I stopped fixating on the single branch that wasn't working out, and looked instead at the larger limb it grew from — and then at the whole tree.

That's when my godmother, Amy Woodroof Moss, asked

me, "How do you know so much, Gabriel?" I didn't quite know how to answer her — so I started writing. I began analyzing myself, my habits, my curiosities. That self-analysis is what led to this book. It made me look back not just at who I am now, but at the child who built science projects in the living room and became fascinated with everything. Eventually, that reflection led me to the Interdisciplinary Studies department at my university, where I designed the degree I'm now pursuing: Performance-Based Learning Design. Through the optimistic lens of polymathy (and a bit of guidance along the way), I realized my so-called "scattered interests" were never scattered at all. They were connected. And in that realization, I didn't feel lost anymore. I felt found.

Scarcity and Loss

The pessimist lives in a mindset of scarcity: *"If I learn A, I miss B."*

- If I read this book, I'll never have time to read all the others.
- If I study history, I'll never become good at physics.
- If I spend an evening with friends, I lose the chance to watch that documentary.

Learning becomes a tally of losses, not gains. Every choice is a closed door.

But humans are made to learn. Curiosity should not wound us.

Abundance and Gain

The optimist flips the script: *"If I learn A, it will help me learn B."*

- If I read Book A, it may prepare me for Book B.

- If I study history, I'll understand a context that makes physics more meaningful.

- If I spend an evening with friends, I gain joy and connection — and perhaps we'll watch that documentary together another time.

Learning becomes cumulative, not competitive. Each choice enriches the next.

Reframing Curiosity as a Path, Not a Trap

The point of learning is to grow, and you cannot grow if you see every choice as a loss. Children understand this instinctively.

When a child wants to try something, they don't ask: *"What will I miss by doing this?"* They simply try. If they like it, they keep going. If not, they stop. Either way, they've gained.

That's how we should approach learning: not as a trap, but as a path.

"That's how we should approach learning: not as a trap but as a path."

A Polymath's Perspective

Polymaths especially must embrace the abundance mindset. The pessimist sees "too much to learn" and freezes. The optimist sees "too much to learn" and celebrates.

- The pessimist dreads their ignorance.

- The optimist treasures their ignorance — because it means there will always be something new to discover.

The pessimist looks at a forest and despairs at how many trees there are. The optimist enters the same forest and says: *"Wonderful. I will never run out of paths to walk."*

Closing Thought
 The smartest people are not those who finish the most books or master the most fields. They are the ones who can turn every choice into a gain, every step into part of the path.

There will always be more trees in the forest than you can climb. Celebrate that. For a polymath, abundance is not the enemy — it is the gift.

Polymath Prompt: Reframe a Scarcity Thought

Think of a time you said to yourself: *"If I do A, I'll miss B."*

Now flip it: *"If I do A, I'll be better prepared for B."*

Notice how the same situation feels lighter — more abundant, less constrained.

The Polymath's Path

_____

_____

_____

_____

_____

_____

_____

_____

_____

_____

_____

_____

_____

_____

_____

_____

_____

_____

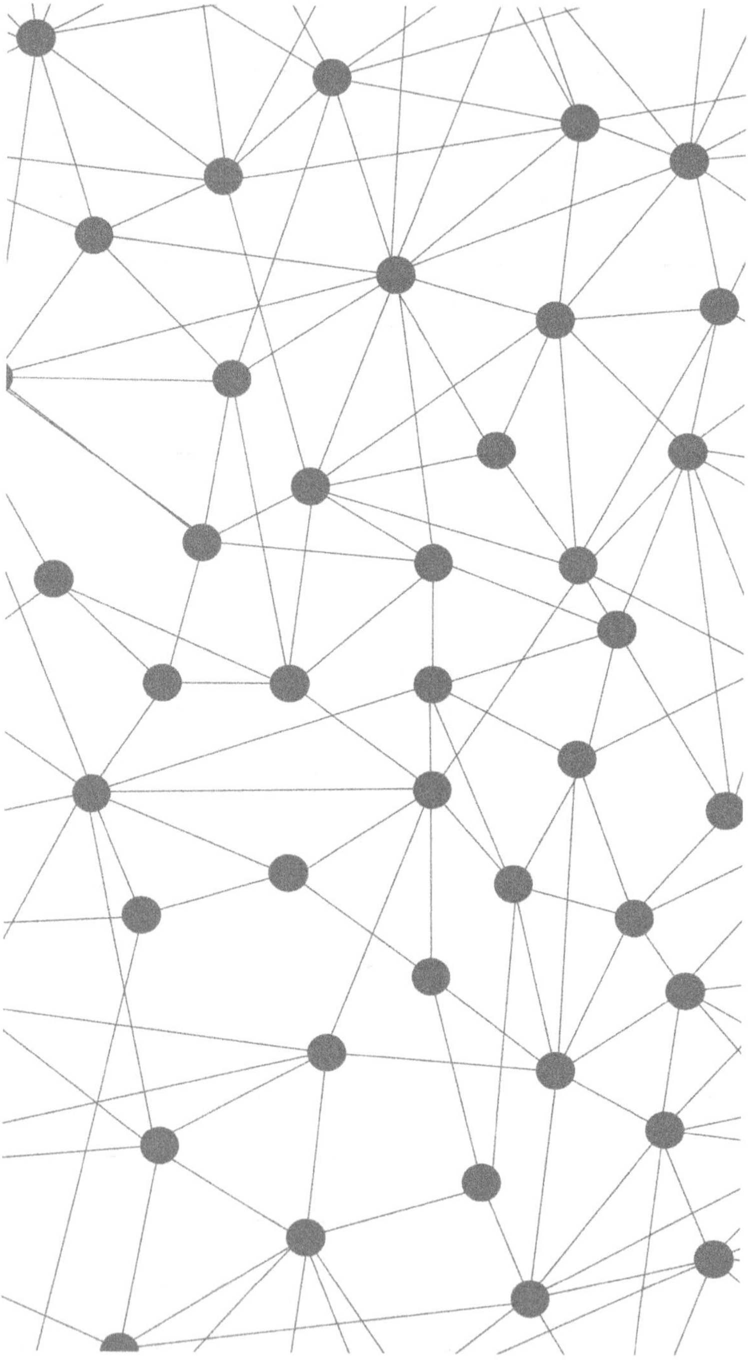

CHAPTER 4:

THE IMPORTANCE OF HOBBIES

The Importance of Hobbies

Rest, Renewal, and Entry Points to Learning

When I was fourteen, I became fascinated with wild plants and what could be done with them. I was a big fan of the *Survivor Man* series from Les Stroud as a kid, and his adventures inspired me to learn more.

That spark of curiosity led me into bushcraft and survival by the time I was sixteen. I studied how to build emergency shelters, make fire, purify water, find food in nature, and identify medicinal plants. From there, my interests grew into looking at how old civilizations thrived with what they had at hand.

In 2021, during the height of the COVID-19 pandemic, I discovered two certification courses — one in **herbal medicine** and another in **Curanderismo**, the traditional folk healing of Meso-America. Both were university-backed, both deeply aligned with the path I had been on since I was a teenager.

If it weren't for those hobbies — the small choices to spend time outside, to study plants, to test bushcraft skills — I would never have discovered the professional opportunities and knowledge I hold today.

When people ask, "What do you do for fun?" too often the answer is work, study, or nothing at all. But hobbies are not trivial. They are the fuel of curiosity, the buffer against burnout, and often the entry points into lifelong interests.

The Four Types of Hobbies

Most people naturally drift toward hobbies in four categories:

- **Intellectual** – The pursuit of understanding. Reading philosophy, learning a language, solving puzzles, studying astronomy.

- **Creative** – The act of shaping something new. Writing poetry, painting, composing music, gardening.

- **Physical** – The use of the body to strengthen and sustain life. Running, yoga, swimming, martial arts.

- **Social** – The integration of the individual into a group. Hosting dinners, joining a club, playing team sports, volunteering.

"...you are more than your obligations."

You Don't Need Four Separate Hobbies

Here's the best news: you don't need one in each category. Some hobbies overlap naturally.

- **Tennis** covers physical and social.

- **Poetry** is both creative and intellectual.

- **Escape rooms** combine intellectual, physical, and social in one experience.

If you don't have the time or energy for four distinct

hobbies, look for ones that serve multiple needs.

Why Hobbies Matter

A hobby takes you out of the continuous taxation of life. Without them, people fall into crisis:

- **Empty nesters and retirees** often sink into dismal states when their lives lack meaningful hobbies.
- **Overworked adults** face midlife crises when they only work and never play.
- **Students** who make study their entire identity often burn out, losing passion and perspective.

Hobbies prevent this. They give your mind and body rest, renewal, and joy. They open conversations that move beyond the daily grind. They remind you that you are more than your obligations.

Hobbies as Entry Points

For polymaths, hobbies are not just leisure — they are *entry points.*

It can be daunting to decide which subjects to pursue seriously. A hobby offers a way to test the waters without pressure.

- At worst, you gain a skill and a story.
- At best, you uncover a new path that becomes part of your forest of learning.

The Polymath's Path

Many great pursuits begin as hobbies. Today's casual experiment could become tomorrow's lifelong study. And if you don't pursue a hobby, you are left with an appreciation for what it takes to do that hobby.

Closing Thought

Hobbies are not distractions from real life — they are the practices that give real life its spark. For the polymath, hobbies are the soil where curiosity grows, the spaces where you rest and renew, and the paths where new trees first take root.

Polymath Prompt: Identify Your Entry Point

Think of one hobby you've carried for years. How has it grown — into a branch, a tree, or even a forest?

Now think of one new hobby you've always wanted to try. What category would it fall into — and what new path might it open?

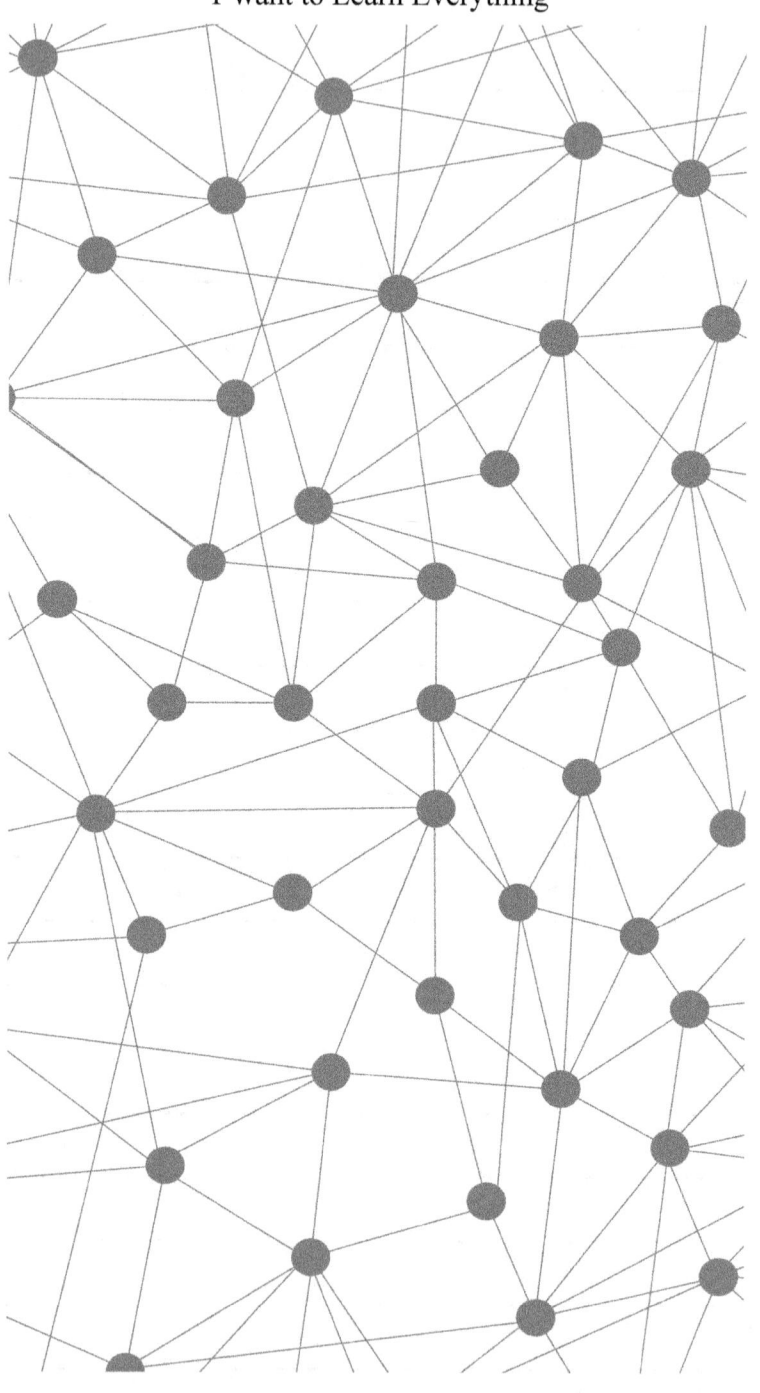

CHAPTER 5:

KNOWING HOW MUCH YOU DON'T KNOW

Knowing How Much You Don't Know

Humility as the Gateway to Growth

My grandfather used to say:

> *"Someone who has been in a place for three weeks knows everything about that place. Someone who has been there three months understands they know very little."*

He meant it about travel, but the lesson applies far more widely. The same is true for learning any skill or field.

The Timeline of Learning

I've often reflected on my grandfather's words and added my own extension:

- **Three weeks:** Someone with three weeks of experience feels confident, almost certain. They believe they know everything worth knowing.

- **Three months:** With more time, cracks appear. They realize they don't know that much yet. Confidence gives way to humility.

*Between three months and a year is the toughest part. You will feel resistance as your mind rewires to learn and grow with what you're learning–this is where many people give up, the trick is to be **resilient** and **power through** this time.*

- **One year:** Now the learner begins to know what they don't know. They can identify gaps, recognize blind spots, and know where to look for answers.

- **Three years:** At this stage, the learner can begin piecing together solutions themselves, building new insights out of what they've already learned.

This cycle repeats at every level of mastery. The deeper you go, the more vast the field becomes.

Humility in Polymathy

The habit of a polymath is living in this awareness across multiple domains. You often know more than people expect — and sometimes more than you let on — but you also recognize how much remains beyond your grasp.

That awareness brings a profound humility. You come to see that *anyone* — from the master of their craft to the youngest child — has something to teach you.

Humility is not self-deprecation. It's an openness that makes the world infinitely more interesting.

"...be resilient and power through this..."

Awareness Over Certainty

Certainty closes conversations. Awareness keeps them alive.

Most people enjoy dialogue, not lectures. They'd rather share stories, trade perspectives, and puzzle things out together than be handed a definitive answer. As a polymath, you may carry deep knowledge across many subjects, but resist the temptation to turn every interaction into a display of certainty.

Instead, lean into curiosity. Use your knowledge as a bridge, not a shield. Let others surprise you.

Closing Thought
Knowledge is not a mountain to be conquered; it's a horizon that expands the closer you walk to it. The more you learn, the more you discover you don't know. Embrace that. For the polymath, humility is not a limitation — it is the gateway to endless growth.

Polymath Prompt: Humility in Action

Think of a subject you know fairly well. Now ask yourself:

- What are three things you still don't understand about it?

- Who might you learn from — even if they seem unlikely?

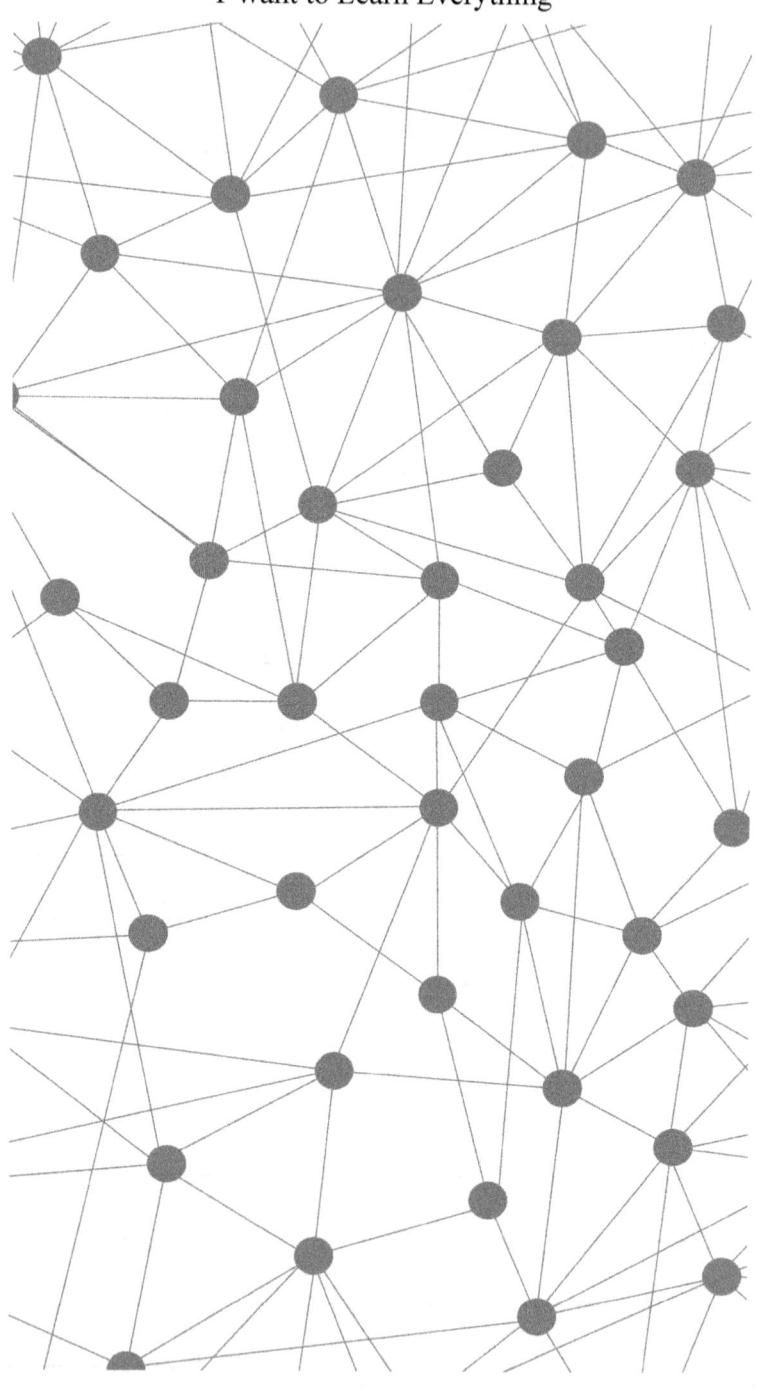

CHAPTER 6:

THE TRUE ART OF DISCUSSION

The True Art of Discussion

Building Respect Before Persuasion

When I was a teenager, I was very set in my understanding of things — as most young people are. Looking back now, it astounds me how much easier my life could have been if I had simply listened to the advice offered by the people around me: parents, friends, mentors. I think this is an experience many can share.

We often learn the hard way that listening is not the same as hearing. Hearing registers words. Listening absorbs meaning. And understanding requires a deeper step still — setting aside our need to be right long enough to truly consider another person's perspective.

My speech and debate professor Brandan Whearty once told us:

> *"Anyone can listen to opinions that support their own, but I'll always respect the person who takes the time to not only listen to the opposing side but try and understand the opposing side."*

That single line changed how I listen.

Listening to Understand, Not Win

Most people enter discussions as if they were contests: I have my position, you have yours, and the goal is to beat you.

But when you listen only to win, you miss the chance to grow.

The true art of discussion is not debate as conquest but dialogue as collaboration. It is about asking:

- Why do you believe this?
- What experiences brought you here?
- What am I not seeing?

When you listen this way, discussion becomes less of a threat and more of a discovery.

"...listening is not the same as hearing."

Respect Over Agreement

That same professor also told us:

> *"When discussing and debating with someone, or giving a speech, the goal isn't to get everyone on your side. The goal is to get everyone to respect your opinion and move a step closer to your understanding."*

Respect is a higher aim than victory. People rarely change their entire worldview in one conversation — but they can leave respecting the way you spoke, the care you showed, and the openness of your mind.

I Want to Learn Everything

That respect often lasts longer than agreement.

Building Bridges Through Dialogue

Every conversation is an opportunity to build a bridge. Not all bridges will be crossed, but the very act of building them expands your world.

For polymaths, this is especially important. You will carry knowledge across many fields, and with that knowledge comes responsibility. If you treat conversation as performance, you close doors. If you treat it as dialogue, you open them.

The goal is not to prove yourself right but to create a space where ideas can move freely — where both you and the other person leave with more than you started.

Closing Thought
The true art of discussion is not about conquering your opponent. It is about cultivating mutual respect, learning through dialogue, and recognizing that even disagreement can strengthen the web of understanding between people.

Polymath Prompt: Try the Respect Approach

Think of a recent conversation where you disagreed with someone. Ask yourself:

- Did you listen to win, or to understand?

- If you framed your goal as earning respect rather than victory, how would that change the way you approached it?

I Want to Learn Everything

_____

_____

_____

_____

_____

_____

_____

_____

_____

_____

_____

_____

_____

_____

_____

_____

_____

_____

_____

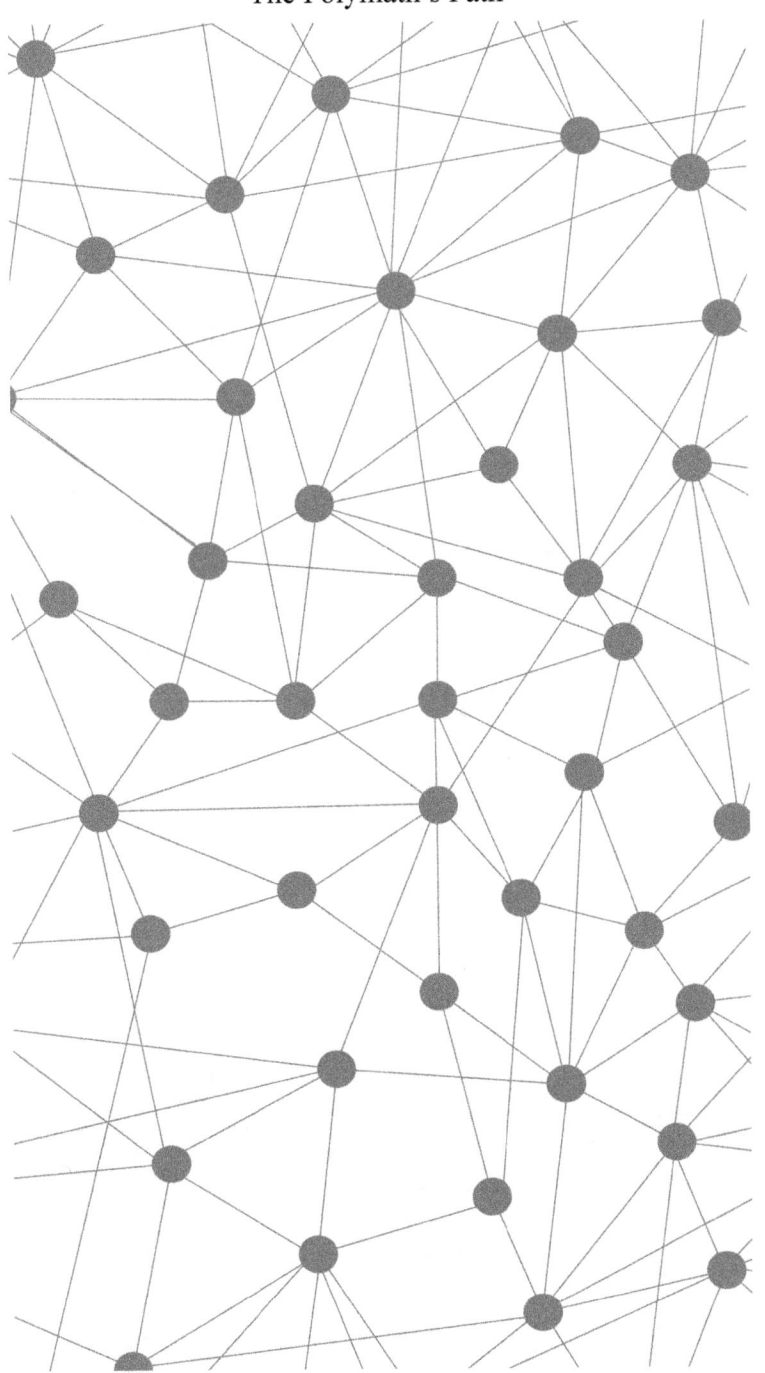

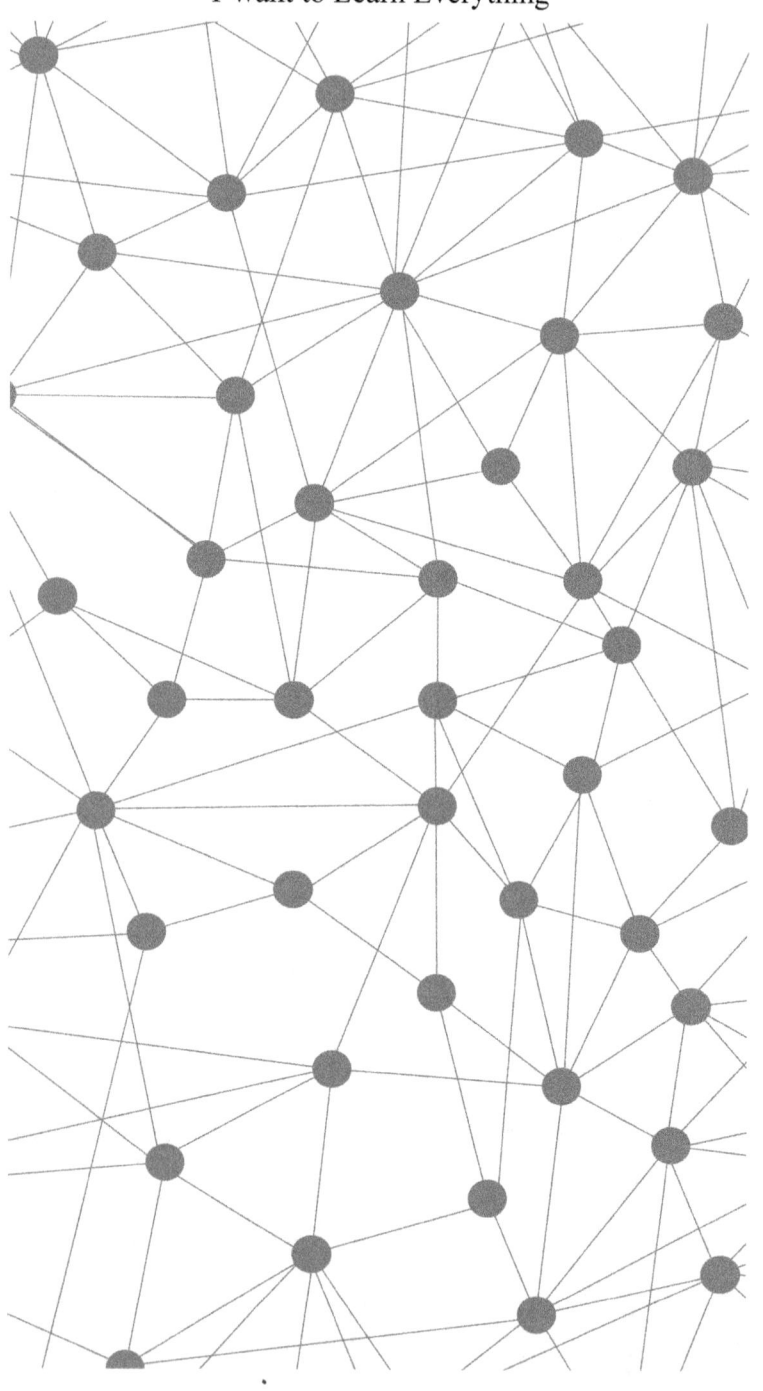

CHAPTER 7:

KNOWLEDGE IS A GROWING LANDSCAPE

Knowledge Is a Growing Landscape

Walking Beyond the Horizon

When you first begin learning something new, it feels like standing in a small clearing. Everything around you seems visible, contained, and understandable. You might even think: *"I can see the whole field."*

But as you walk further, the landscape grows. The horizon stretches. More paths open. What once looked like the edge of the map reveals new valleys, mountains, and rivers waiting to be explored.

Knowledge works the same way. The more you learn, the more you realize how much more there is to learn. The map doesn't shrink. It expands.

The Map Gets Bigger the Further You Walk

At first, knowledge feels finite. But with each step, the boundaries widen.

- A beginner at painting may think there are only a handful of styles — watercolor, oil, acrylic. After years of practice, they discover endless traditions, methods, and histories hidden beyond the first horizon.

- A student in biology might start by memorizing cell structures, only to realize that each discovery opens into whole fields: genetics, ecology, microbiology, biochemistry.

This isn't discouragement. It's wonder. The more you walk, the more landscape there is to see.

"...learning is not just about gathering facts. It's about sharing maps with one another..."

Sharing Maps: The Value of Perspective

One of the most powerful aspects of being human is that we don't explore the landscape alone. Each of us draws our own mental map, shaped by the paths we've walked.

- Someone who studies physics may draw a terrain of laws and forces.
- Someone who studies music may map the world in rhythms and harmonies.
- Someone who studies culture may map it in traditions, rituals, and stories.

When we share perspectives, it's like comparing maps. Each map shows the same world, but with different features highlighted. The physicist can help the musician see patterns of resonance; the musician can help the physicist hear the music in the math.

The more maps we share, the richer our collective landscape becomes.

My own family has always practiced this instinctively. Wherever we go — a zoological or botanical garden, a museum, an art exhibit — we stop to read every plaque and sign, soaking up information like sponges. Friends and teachers often remark on it.

Sometimes, we make it a game. On a visit to the Prado in Spain, we decided each person would pick one piece, read about it in detail, and then present it to the rest of the group. We walked together from artwork to artwork, taking turns as guides, discussing and comparing what we had learned.

Another time, on a road trip through the U.S., we stopped at the small historical town of Fort Stockton. We discovered there was a driving tour with plaques marking significant sites. What could have been a quick stop became a three-hour journey into the town's history — every plaque read, every story discussed.

For us, learning is not just about gathering facts. It's about sharing maps with one another, and in doing so, expanding the terrain for everyone.

Growing Together

Learning doesn't happen in isolation. Just as no tree grows alone in the forest, our intellectual roots thrive when they intertwine with others. Conversations, friendships, mentorships—each acts like mycorrhizal threads that pass nutrients between trees. Sometimes, one mind feeds another until both are strong enough to stand on their own.

Education researcher Dr. Stephen Krashen described something called the Affective Filter Hypothesis: the idea that emotional barriers—fear, shame, stress—can block the flow of learning. When we lower these filters through kindness, curiosity, and nonjudgment, knowledge passes freely between people.

This is why open dialogue and humility matter so much. When we create a safe environment for growth, others' roots can reach our own. We share energy through encouragement, patience, and empathy. Sometimes, we're the tree with deep roots sharing our nutrients. Other times, we're the one on the rock, relying on the strength of others until we can grow into the soil ourselves.

True connection—between people or ideas—always accelerates growth. The forest flourishes when every tree contributes to the canopy.

The Underground Network

Beneath every thriving forest lies an unseen web: roots, fungi, water channels, and electrical signals all exchanging information and nutrients. Our brains and societies work the same way. Every conversation, every idea, every act of learning adds another thread to the network.

When two ideas seem completely unrelated—like trees standing far apart—it's tempting to see them as separate. But if you study each deeply enough, their roots begin to grow toward each other. Eventually, the connection becomes clear, and both ideas nourish one another.

Polymathic thinking is the deliberate practice of cultivating these connections. It's the art of extending roots into new territories of thought until your inner ecosystem becomes diverse, resilient, and alive.

So when learning feels slow, remember: the roots are working. The forest is growing underground.

I Want to Learn Everything
Asking Better Questions Over Time

In the early stages of learning, we ask simple questions: *"What is this? How does it work?"* These are good starting points, but as the landscape expands, so do our questions.

- A novice cook asks: "How do I bake bread?"
- An experienced baker asks: "Why does fermentation behave differently in different climates?"
- A master baker asks: "What can bread teach us about culture, chemistry, and history?"

The depth of our questions reflects how far we've walked. A growing map doesn't just give us answers — it teaches us to ask better questions.

Closing Thought
Knowledge is not a destination. It is a landscape — endless, expanding, alive. The more you walk, the more there is to see. The more maps you share, the more beautiful the terrain becomes. For the polymath, this is not a burden but a gift: to know that the horizon will never end.

Polymath Prompt: Map Your Landscape

Think of one subject you've been learning. Draw (literally or in your mind) a "map" of what you know: the basics, the landmarks, the gaps.

Then ask yourself: *What lies beyond the horizon? What's the next question I should be asking?*

The Polymath's Path

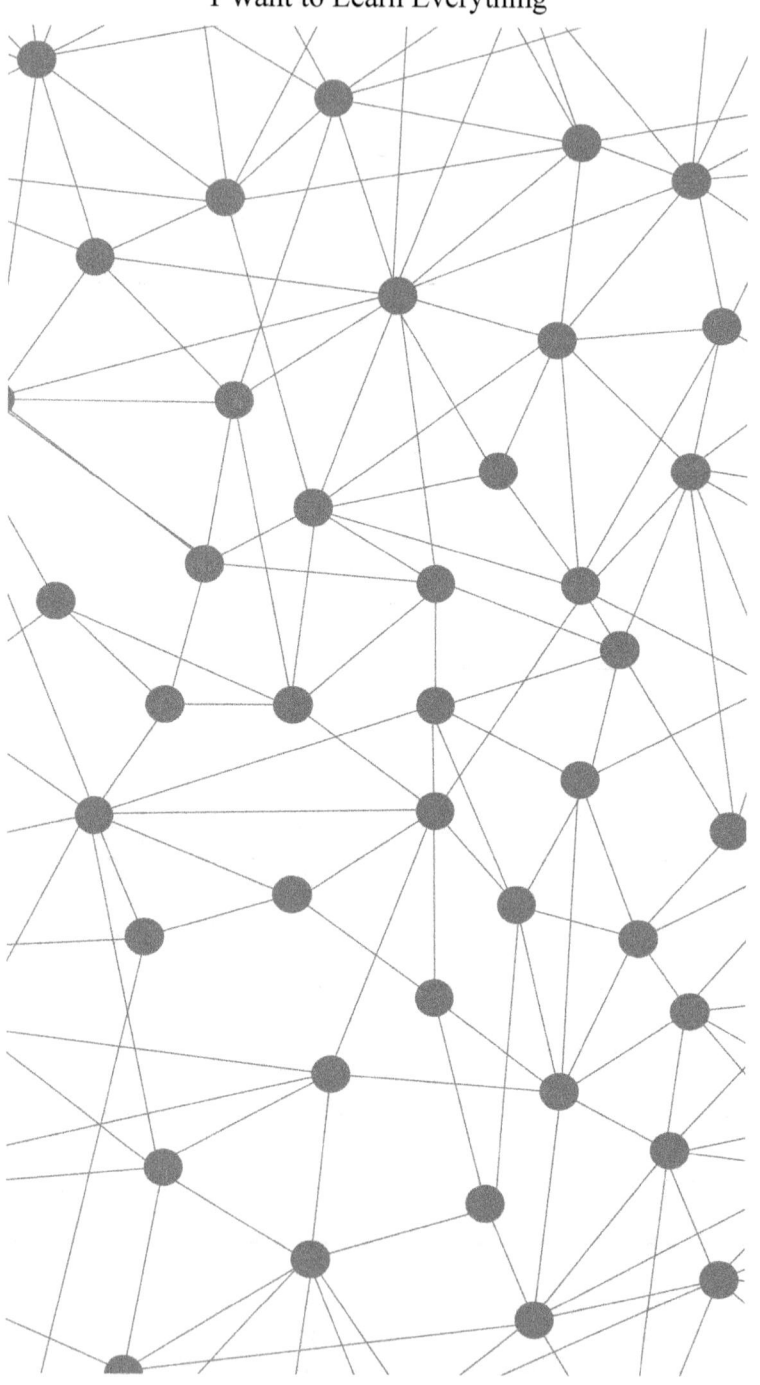

CHAPTER 8:
LEARN IT BY TEACHING IT

Learn It by Teaching It

The Joy of Sharing What You Know

There's a saying in education: *"If you can't explain it simply, you don't understand it well enough."*

One of the best ways to learn isn't just by reading or studying quietly, but by teaching. When you explain something to someone else, you sharpen your own grasp of it. Your mind is forced to organize the information, clarify the details, and confront the gaps.

This is why discussion has always been one of humanity's greatest tools for learning — from salons and symposiums to family dinner tables.

Discussion as a Learning Tool

Research on learning shows that summarizing information in your own words and then teaching it to others improves memory and comprehension.

When you share knowledge, you don't just repeat what you read — you process it, translate it, and embody it. And when you discuss it with others, you expose yourself to new perspectives, corrections, and connections you may have missed.

The "So Basically..." Habit

In my family, this became a cherished habit. Whether

at the dinner table, in a museum, or walking through a garden, we would often get caught up in questions none of us fully knew the answers to.

The ritual was simple: someone would look up the information, read it verbatim, and then say, *"So basically..."* before rephrasing it in their own words.

Then everyone else would take a turn: *"So basically..."* — their own summary, their own angle. If someone misunderstood, the group could clarify. If someone added a unique perspective, it enriched the discussion.

It turned casual learning into a game. But it was also serious practice: the art of turning knowledge into understanding.

"...expose yourself to new perspectives, corrections, and connections..."

The Counting Sheep Adage

There's another exercise I use when I'm on my own. The old advice to "count sheep" to fall asleep isn't really about the sheep. It's about mental pacing.

Try this: *pick a subject you think you know well. From the beginning of your understanding to the furthest reaches, start explaining everything you know, step by step, as if you're counting sheep.*

This practice forces you to notice the holes in your knowledge. It also moves what you *do* know more firmly into memory.

The Socratic Spiral

The philosopher Socrates gave us another timeless method: asking questions to test knowledge. The Socratic method isn't about proving someone wrong — it's about unraveling loose threads until you see what holds and what doesn't.

Each question clarifies. Each answer strengthens or humbles. Done well, it doesn't lead to perfection but to a spiral of deeper understanding.

Closing Thought
Teaching is not the end of learning — it is part of it. The act of sharing knowledge deepens your grasp, reveals your blind spots, and connects you to others. For the polymath, teaching is not a performance of mastery but a practice of growth.

Polymath Prompt: Teach It Out Loud

Choose one subject you've learned recently. Without notes, try explaining it out loud as if to a curious friend.

- Where do you stumble?
- What do you realize you don't fully understand?
- What came out clearer once you spoke it?

I Want to Learn Everything

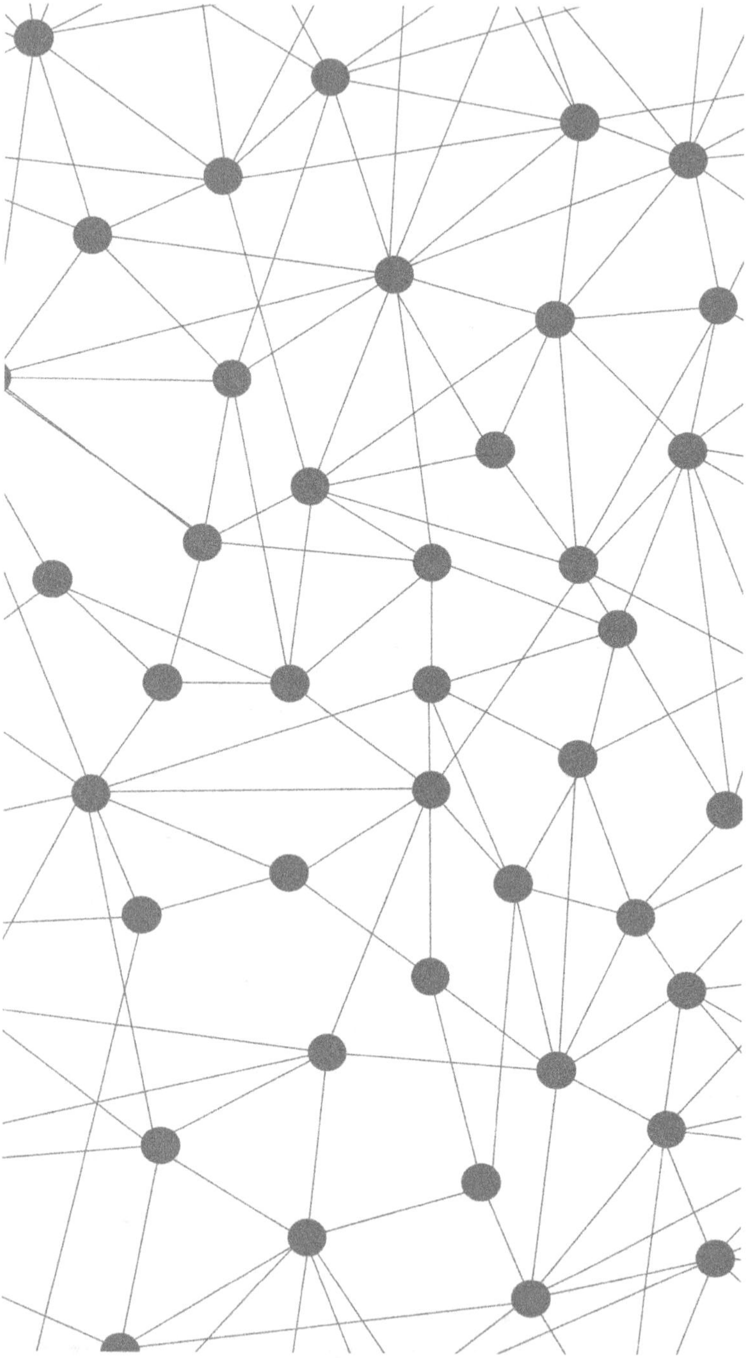

CHAPTER 9:

PAPER MEMORY
A NOTEBOOK GUIDE

Paper Memory — A Notebook Guide

Building a Second Brain

The human brain is capable of astonishing feats. But in the modern world, our attention is constantly under attack. Notifications, endless feeds, and information overload stretch our focus thinner than ever.

I'm not here to lecture about how technology is "ruining memory." Instead, I want to share how we can *strengthen* our memory and free our minds to focus where it matters.

The answer is deceptively simple: build a **Second Brain.**

The Second Brain

A second brain is any system outside your head that stores and organizes information so your mind can think more clearly. For some, that's a notebook. For others, it's an index card box, a digital app, or a binder full of quotes.

For polymaths, second brains are essential. They let you:

- Store information for later review.
- Track ideas as they move from raw thought to developed insight.
- Free up mental space by externalizing details.
- Notice patterns in your own curiosity over time.

The Polymath's Path

Almost every professional field uses a form of second brain — scientists with lab notebooks, architects with sketchbooks, musicians with composition journals. There's nothing stopping you from building your own.

"...handwriting strengthens memory..."

The Notebook Forms

Over the centuries, learners have developed many styles of notebooks. Each has its own strengths:

- **Catch-All Notebook** – A pocket-sized companion for jotting down quick thoughts, overheard phrases, questions, or sketches. Messy, chaotic, but alive.

- **Journal** – A space for reflection. Tracks growth, emotions, and daily experiences. More personal and deliberate than the catch-all.

- **Zibaldone** – A Renaissance-style "scrapbook of thought." Quotes, half-formed ideas, lists, fragments. The middle ground between raw notes and a structured book.

- **Commonplace Book** – A curated log of the best ideas you encounter: passages from books, diagrams, metaphors, recipes, observations. A personal anthology.

- **Compendium** – Your own textbook. A synthesis of knowledge from one or several subjects, written as if to teach someone else.

Together, these forms can carry you through every stage of

learning — from initial spark to eventual mastery.

Why Writing by Hand Matters

One of my humanities professors (Bruce Naschak) insisted on a strict no-electronics rule in class. At first, it felt archaic. But he explained why: when you write something by hand, you don't just record it — you encode it.

Research shows that handwriting strengthens memory, comprehension, and problem-solving.

- Writing is slower than typing, which forces you to process information instead of transcribing it.

- The motor memory of forming letters creates a tactile imprint in the brain.

- Summarizing by hand helps you decide what's important.

My professor was right. Over time, I noticed how much more I remembered — not just the words, but the concepts behind them.

Closing Thought
Your mind is fertile soil, but it cannot hold everything. A notebook is not a crutch — it is a garden bed. It lets your ideas take root, grow, and intertwine over time. For the polymath, the second brain is not optional. It is the scaffolding that allows the forest of knowledge to thrive.

Polymath Prompt: Carry and Capture

For one week, keep something with you to write in. When an idea, fact, or question comes up, write it down. Each evening, review your notes.

Next step: Try shaping these notes into a journal, zibaldone, commonplace book, or compendium.

I Want to Learn Everything

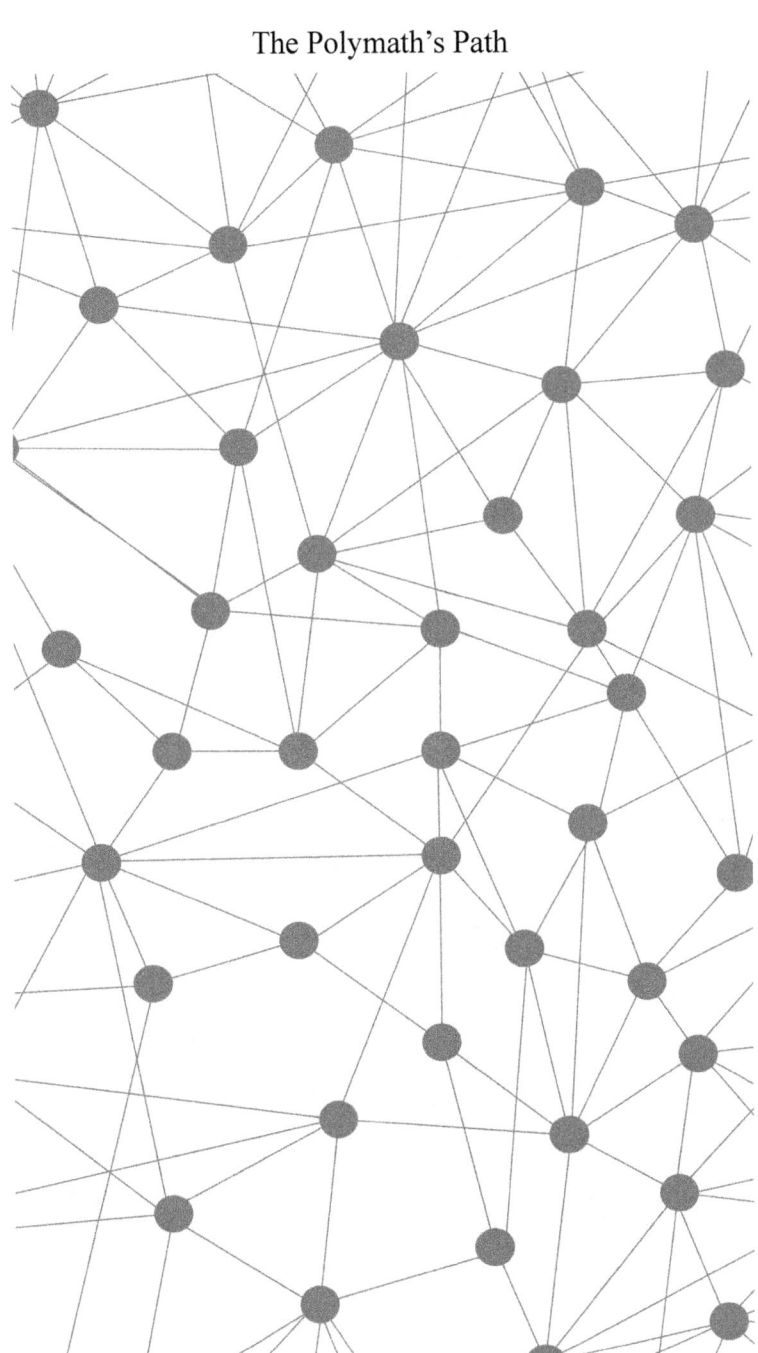

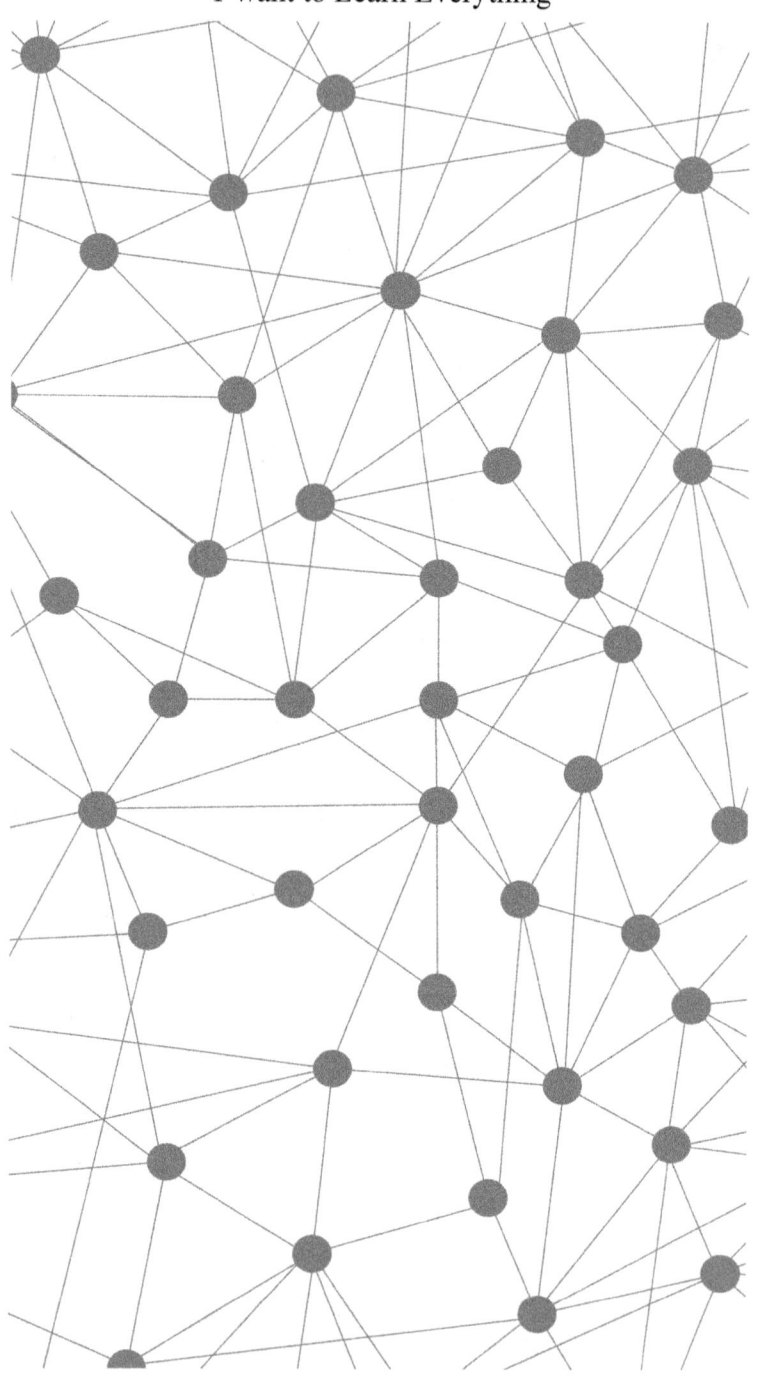

CHAPTER 10:

NEUROPLASTICITY & THE NEVER-LATE BRAIN

Neuroplasticity & the Never-Late Brain

Why Your Mind Can Always Grow

Opening: Growth Beyond the Timeline

At 25, I'm finishing my bachelor's degree — about 3–4 years later than most of my U.S. university peers. By conventional standards, I might seem "behind". My frontal lobe is fully formed, and my pathways aren't as malleable as those of younger students. Yet I keep learning. I keep growing. My Nana was 42 when she returned to school and got her bachelors in kinesiology and anatomy. My mother is 55 and learning French and making connections to spanish and english. There is no timeline to learning.

That's because learning isn't limited by age — it's a lifelong ability. Neuroplasticity ensures that, no matter where you start, your brain can still adapt, expand, and flourish.

Brain Rewiring Through Challenge and Novelty

Your brain isn't static — it reshapes itself continuously. When faced with new challenges or information, your neurons connect, reinforce, and sometimes grow anew. This is the essence of neuroplasticity (Lövdén et al., 2010).

Novelty is especially potent — new experiences trigger dopamine pathways, strengthening focus and memory. Enriched environments, physical activity, and intellectually stimulating contexts promote synaptogenesis and even cortical thickening (Park & Bischof, 2013).

Micro-Learning and the Daily Wiring of the Brain

If neuroplasticity is the brain's ability to rewire itself, then *Information Sampling* is how we hand it the raw material to do so.

Every new piece of information you encounter — a sentence from a book, a line of poetry, a diagram, a song lyric — acts as a spark that encourages new neural pathways to form. Small, steady exposure to ideas keeps the mind flexible, active, and awake to connection.

The key is scale. The brain thrives on short, varied stimulation — not constant overload. Just as muscles grow stronger through regular micro-tension, neurons strengthen through regular micro-learning. Sampling five minutes of something new each day can be more transformative than cramming for hours once a week.

This approach also lowers what linguist Steven Krashen calls the affective filter — the emotional barrier that blocks learning when we feel anxious or judged. Sampling is gentle. It creates safety in curiosity. You allow information to come to you, not demand mastery from yourself immediately.

Like tasting a new spice or hearing a new accent, each encounter reshapes the map of what your mind recognizes and values. Over time, your brain begins to find harmony between far-flung ideas — the same way roots, given time and space, eventually find one another beneath the soil.

"...learning has no deadline."

Why It's Never Too Late to Learn

Neuroplasticity persists through adulthood. Studies show that learning new skills later in life—like languages, music, or technology—is associated with slower cognitive decline and may delay dementia (Stern, 2012).

Even in adults in their 60s and 70s, combining physical activity, mental stimulation, and a healthy diet has shown measurable improvements in cognitive performance, as if the brain were 1–2 years younger (Ngandu et al., 2015).

Researchers have also found that education and continued learning contribute significantly to **cognitive reserve**, providing resilience against brain aging and neurodegeneration (Snowdon et al., 1996; Stern, 2012).

Growth Through Repetition, Sleep, and Reflection

Three habitual anchors—repetition, rest, and reflection—supercharge learning:

- **Repetition** strengthens neural pathways.
- **Rest** consolidates learning and repairs brain circuits.
- **Reflection** (through review or writing) helps internalize and integrate what we have absorbed.

These practices aren't new — but they're your brain's best

allies, at any age.

Closing Thought
Age doesn't limit curiosity — it shapes it. Neuroplasticity shows us that our brains remain capable of growth, no matter when we begin. You are never too late to learn, never too slow to evolve. Every new skill is living proof that human learning has no deadline.

Polymath Prompt: Try Something New

Choose one small new skill or topic. Practice it intentionally for a week. Notice the way your mind responds — what's easier, what connects?

I Want to Learn Everything

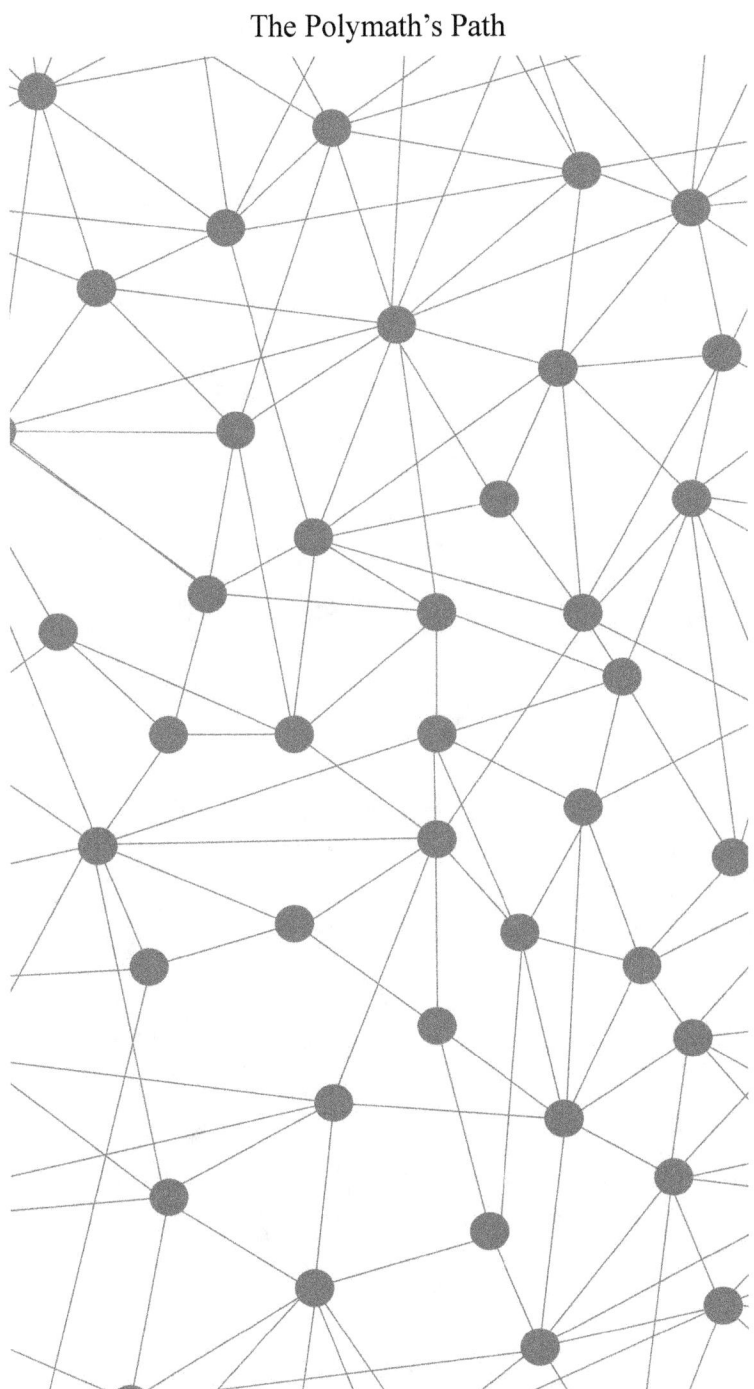

I Want to Learn Everything

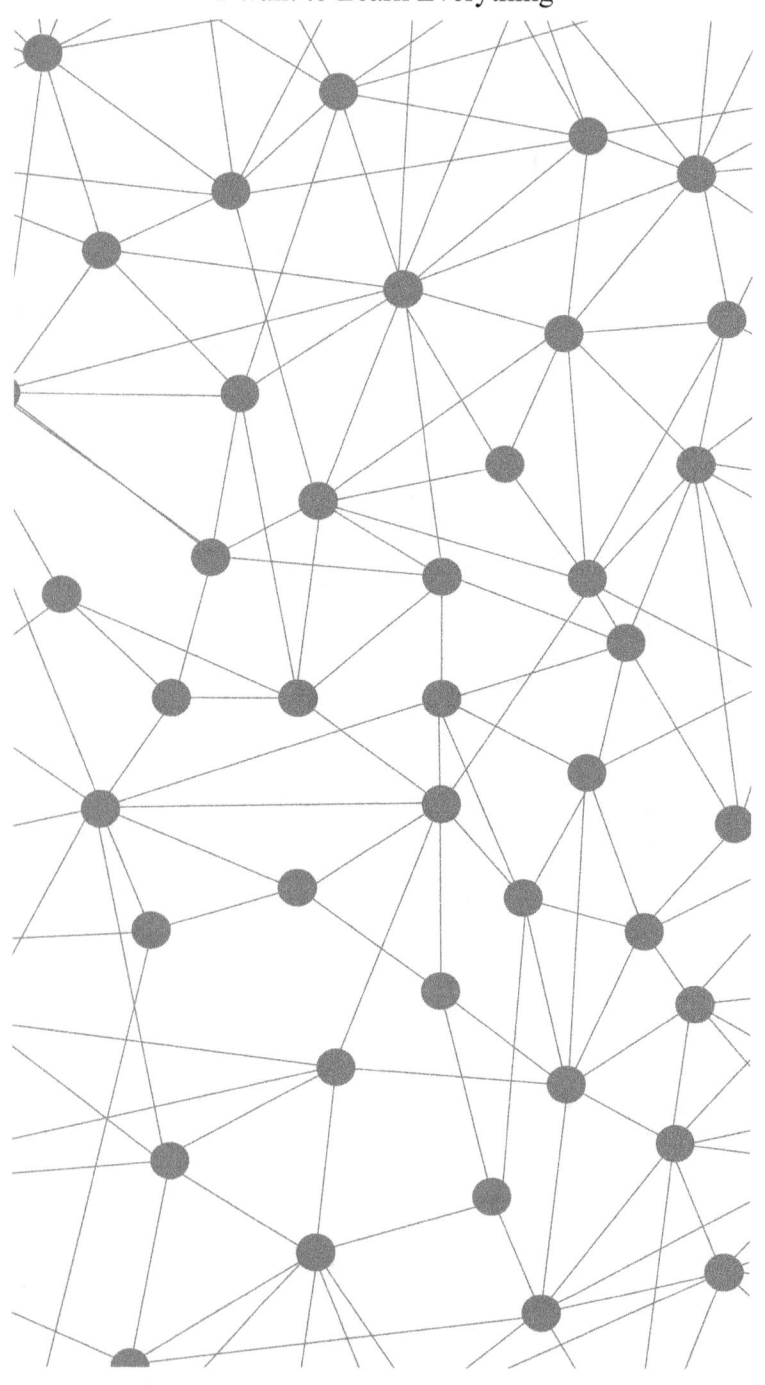

CHAPTER 11:

THE PHYSICAL TOOLKIT (EVERYDAY CARRY)

The Physical Toolkit (Everyday Carry)

Equipping Curiosity and Conversation

When I walk out the door, I like to know I'm ready for whatever the day brings. Not just the expected — classes, errands, work — but the surprises. A spontaneous conversation, an idea that needs capturing, a friend inviting me out.

That's why I carry a small toolkit with me at all times. It isn't about survival gear or high-tech gadgets. It's about readiness: being able to write, to share, to connect, and to adapt.

Why Carry an EDC as a Polymath?

Every polymath needs a **second brain** (Chapter 9), but also a set of tools that make curiosity portable. An EDC (Everyday Carry) does three things:

1. **Captures ideas** before they slip away.
2. **Opens opportunities** for connection and conversation.
3. **Signals preparedness** — to yourself and to others.

When you expect ideas and connections to arrive, you're always ready to meet them.

The Polymath's Path

"Curiosity often arrives unannounced."

What I Carry (and Why)

- **Pen** – Because the brain remembers what the hand writes.
- **Pocket notebook (in a leather case)** – My catch-all for raw ideas, overheard phrases, quick sketches, or sudden sparks. Inside:
  - A few 3×5 cards (for notes to give away).
  - Extra business/brand cards (to share who I am).
- **Wallet** – More than money:
  - Business cards for professional connections.
  - Personal "brand" cards for deeper conversations.
  - A bottle opener — because hospitality often begins with small gestures.
- **Analog watch** – Keeps me aware of time without pulling me into distractions on my phone. Also: timeless elegance.
- **Phone** – A tool, not a trap. Photos, quick research, voice memos, translation.
- **Handkerchief** – Simple, old-world utility. For spills, kindness, or just a touch of refinement.

This isn't about impressing anyone. It's about being ready for the small moments that matter.

Closing Thought

A toolkit doesn't make you a polymath. But it gives you the readiness to live like one. Curiosity often arrives unannounced. Be ready to write it down, share it, or welcome it in. Sometimes, the smallest tools make the biggest difference.

Polymath Prompt: Pack Your Toolkit

For one week, carry something — anything — that makes you more prepared to capture or connect. A pen. A small notebook. An extra card. Look at your day and think about one thing that you need often, and take it with you in the morning to see if it proves handy.

At the end of the week, ask: *How did being prepared change my days?*

End Section One

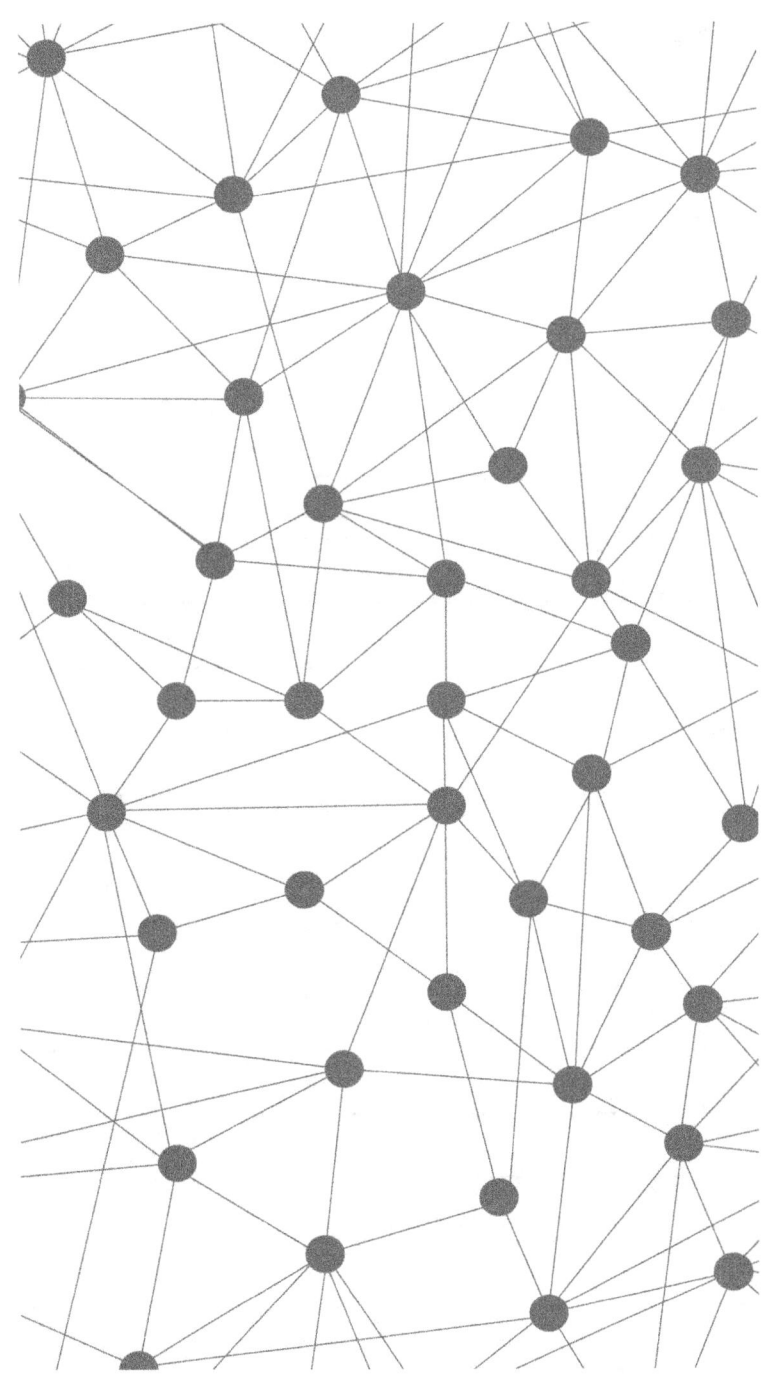

Notes:

Interlude Appendix: Tool-to-Discipline Crosswalk

How to Apply Toolkit Skills to the Disciplines

One of the challenges of polymathy is knowing how to use your learning tools in different fields. The same skill — note-taking, discussion, or teaching — takes on new shapes depending on the subject. This guide offers a crosswalk between the tools from Section One and the disciplines from Section Two.

Language Learning

- **Handwriting** – Write new words by hand for stronger recall.

- **Spaced Repetition** – Review vocabulary at increasing intervals.

- **Active Recall** – Quiz yourself instead of rereading.

- **Discussion** – Practice with others to build fluency.

- **Catch-All Notebook** – Record phrases you encounter "in the wild."

Art & Music

- **Zibaldone** – Collect sketches, fragments, or lyrics in progress.

- **Commonplace Book** – Save inspiring quotes, scores, or visual motifs.

- **Synthesis** – Blend styles, genres, or media into new forms.

- **Compendium** – Build your own "manual" of

- techniques and studies.
- **Observation Practice** – Train your eye and ear by analyzing works.

Math & Science

- **Teach-It Method** – Explain concepts out loud ("So basically...").
- **Sketching & Diagrams** – Draw problems, processes, or systems.
- **Discussion** – Share and debate theories with peers.
- **Reflection Journal** – Track experiments and insights.
- **Counting Sheep Adage** – Recall everything you know step by step.

History & Society

- **Commonplace Book** – Copy passages, speeches, and timelines.
- **Discussion Groups** – Test interpretations with others.
- **Socratic Spiral** – Ask "why" questions to dig into causes and effects.
- **Perspective-Sharing** – Compare cultural "maps" across time.
- **Legacy Thinking** – Reflect on lessons for the present.

Health & Fitness

- **Daily Journal** – Track routines, sleep, diet, and progress.
- **Reflection** – Notice emotional and physical connections.
- **Spaced Repetition** – Reinforce exercise form or nutrition knowledge.
- **EDC (Everyday Carry)** – Keep small tools (e.g., notebook, water bottle) for consistency.

Technology & Engineering

- **Sketching** – Diagrams, prototypes, systems thinking.
- **Zibaldone** – Capture fragments of design ideas or code snippets.
- **Teach-It Method** – Explain technical concepts simply.
- **Compendium** – Build a personal guide to tools, formulas, and projects.
- **Discussion** – Collaborate with makers and problem-solvers.

Philosophy & Critical Thinking

- **Socratic Spiral** – Iterative questioning to test assumptions.
- **Reflection Journal** – Record daily questions and insights.
- **Commonplace Book** – Collect arguments, quotes, and definitions.

- **Debate Practice** – Sharpen reasoning with dialogue.
- **Bias Awareness** – Track assumptions in your own notes.

Economics & Business

- **Catch-All Notebook** – Capture ideas and opportunities quickly.
- **Commonplace Book** – Gather business models, case studies, or strategies.
- **Discussion** – Learn through negotiation, pitching, or debate.
- **Teach-It Method** – Practice explaining economic ideas clearly.
- **Compendium** – Draft a personal guide to business concepts.

Nature & Environment

- **Field Journal** – Record observations, sketches, and measurements.
- **Zibaldone** – Collect quotes, fragments, or raw data.
- **Commonplace Book** – Save lessons from ecology, geology, or sustainability texts.
- **Reflection** – Connect field experiences with broader environmental questions.
- **Synthesis** – Combine science, ethics, and design for practical solutions.

Literature & Storytelling

- **Commonplace Book** – Copy favorite passages and story ideas.
- **Zibaldone** – Draft fragments, metaphors, or unfinished pieces.
- **Teach-It Method** – Retell stories in your own words.
- **Discussion** – Share and interpret literature with others.
- **Compendium** – Collect writing exercises, themes, or archetypes.

Spirituality & Self-Understanding

- **Reflection Journal** – Meditations, dreams, and inner dialogue.
- **Legacy Thinking** – Write about values and long-term meaning.
- **Commonplace Book** – Collect myths, parables, or sacred texts.
- **Discussion** – Explore different traditions respectfully.
- **Socratic Spiral** – Use questioning to clarify personal beliefs.

Craft & Design

- **Sketching** – Draft plans, patterns, or design ideas.
- **Zibaldone** – Collect fragments of inspiration (textures, techniques).
- **Compendium** – Write your own "maker's manual" as you practice.

- **Observation Practice** – Study the form and function of well-designed objects.
- **Discussion** – Learn from artisans and peers in workshops or makerspaces.

Closing Thought

The toolkit is not separate from the disciplines — it's woven into them. Every notebook, question, or discussion becomes more powerful when applied directly. Use this crosswalk as a reminder: the tools you already hold can open any door to learning.

Appendices

Appendix A: The Polymath's Lexicon

- **Polymath** – one who pursues both breadth and depth of knowledge across multiple fields.

- **Polyhistor** – an older synonym for polymath, from Greek roots meaning "very learned."

- **Polyglot** – one who speaks four or more languages fluently; a helpful analogy for polymathy.

- **Generalist** – one who spreads knowledge broadly across fields, connecting networks of ideas.

- **Specialist** – one who focuses deeply on a single domain, developing precision and mastery.

- **The Specialist-Generalist Wave** – The recurring cycle between specialization and synthesis that drives collective progress.

- **Forest (of the Mind)** – Metaphor for a polymath's learning: seeds, saplings, trees, interconnected ecosystems.

- **Roots, Trunks, Branches** – breadth, depth, and skills as parts of the forest metaphor.

- **Saplings & Seeds** – emerging interests on the way to becoming pillars or trees.

- **Abundance Mindset** – seeing curiosity as opportunity ("If I learn A, it prepares me for B").

- **Scarcity Mindset** – seeing learning as limitation ("If I learn A, I miss B").

- **Second Brain** – any external system (notebook, digital, cards) that captures and organizes thoughts.

- **Catch-All Notebook** – a pocket-sized tool for raw, unfiltered notes and ideas.

- **Journal** – a space for reflection and growth, more deliberate than a catch-all.

- **Zibaldone** – a Renaissance-style notebook of fragments, quotes, and half-ideas.

- **Commonplace Book** – a curated anthology of the best ideas, quotes, and insights you encounter.

- **Compendium** – a personal textbook; synthesized knowledge written as if to teach others.

- **Everyday Carry (EDC)** – the practical toolkit of items you carry daily for readiness.

- **So Basically… Habit** – the family practice of rephrasing knowledge aloud in simple words to confirm understanding.

- **Socratic Spiral** – asking iterative questions (inspired by Socrates) to deepen understanding and reveal assumptions.

- **Counting Sheep Adage** – recalling everything you know on a subject step by step to test your knowledge.

- **Information Sampling** – A daily micro-learning habit that keeps the brain flexible by exposing it to diverse ideas in brief, consistent bursts.

- **Metacognition** – thinking about thinking; awareness of your learning process.

- **Heuristic** – a mental shortcut or rule of thumb used in problem-solving.

- **Synthesis** – weaving insights from multiple fields into a new whole.

- **Bias** – a lens or blind spot that shapes perception and decision-making.

- **Humility (in Learning)** – recognizing how much you don't know, and staying open to learning from anyone.

- **Perspective-Sharing** – treating dialogue as a comparison of maps that expands collective understanding.

Appendix B: Works Cited & Further Study

Primary Works & Quotes Referenced

- Aurelius, Marcus. *Meditations.*

- Descartes, René. *Discourse on Method.*

- Goethe, Johann Wolfgang von. *Maxims and Reflections.*

- Norton, Richie. Quotation on Michelangelo and creativity.

- Socrates (via Plato). *Apology.*

- Angelou, Maya. *I Know Why the Caged Bird Sings.*

Scientific Studies & Research

- Lövdén, M., Bäckman, L., Lindenberger, U., Schaefer, S., & Schmiedek, F. (2010). *A theoretical framework for the study of adult cognitive plasticity.* Psychological Bulletin, 136(4), 659–676.

- Stern, Y. (2012). *Cognitive reserve in ageing and Alzheimer's disease.* The Lancet Neurology, 11(11), 1006–1012.

- Ngandu, T., Lehtisalo, J., Solomon, A., et al. (2015). *A 2-year multidomain intervention of diet, exercise, cognitive training, and vascular risk monitoring versus control to prevent cognitive decline in at-risk elderly people (FINGER): a randomised controlled*

- *trial.* The Lancet, 385(9984), 2255–2263.

- Park, D. C., & Bischof, G. N. (2013). *The aging mind: Neuroplasticity in response to cognitive training.* Dialogues in Clinical Neuroscience, 15(1), 109–119.

- Snowdon, D. A., Kemper, S. J., Mortimer, J. A., et al. (1996). *Linguistic ability in early life and cognitive function and Alzheimer's disease in late life: Findings from the Nun Study.* JAMA, 275(7), 528–532.

Recommended Resources for Further Study

- Hazlitt, Henry. *Economics in One Lesson.*

- Edwards, Betty. *Drawing on the Right Side of the Brain.*

- Pye, David. *The Nature and Art of Workmanship.*

- Rippetoe, Mark. *Starting Strength.*

- The Great Courses — Lecture series on history, science, and philosophy.

- Khan Academy — Free online lessons across math, science, and humanities.

- Coursera / EdX — Structured online courses in multiple disciplines.

- Open Culture — Free books, lectures, and cultural resources.

In Conversation With...

- **Emilia Wapnick** — *How to Be Everything*
- **David Epstein** — *Range*
- **Robert Greene** — *Mastery*
- **Ken Robinson** — *The Element*
- **Walter Isaacson** — *Leonardo da Vinci*
- **Maria Popova** — *Figuring / The Marginalian*

Additional thanks to:

Jennifer Elbert-Rasmussen
Lars Rasmussen
Amy Woodroof Moss
All my friends
and
All my family

I WANT TO LEARN EVERYTHING:
THE POLYMATH'S PATH

By Gabriel P. Elbert-Rasmussen

The Polymath's Path Expanded Edition

~Coming soon~

SECTION TWO: The Disciplines

A few of the fields of knowledge every polymath can explore — and how to start.

Section Two Foreword:

In Section One, we built the toolkit: the habits, perspectives, and practices that help you think and act like a polymath. In this section, we turn outward — to the great disciplines of human knowledge.

This is not a manual for mastery. It is an invitation to begin. Every subject feels clumsy at first. New words, new rules, new frameworks — they can make you feel lost before you feel capable. That's normal.

Each discipline in this section offers more than knowledge; it cultivates *skills of mind and character*. A polymath doesn't study every subject to master it; they explore fields to develop habits of perception, empathy, precision, and synthesis.

These are not just "hobbies" or "interests." They are ways of thinking that enrich your work, leadership, and life.

The goal here is not to overwhelm you with everything there is to know, but to give you starting steps: approachable ways to dip your toes into each discipline, to spark curiosity, and to help you see how fields connect. Below each discipline, you'll see examples of the **core skills and qualities** that field tends to strengthen — both in daily life and in the workplace.

You don't need to explore every chapter. Start with the ones that catch your interest, and return to the others when the time feels right. Polymathy is not about checking every box — it's about weaving knowledge into your own unique forest.

Continue the Jouney

- **Website / Hub**:
  thepolymathspath.wordpress.com
- **Instagram**:
  @polymaths_path

Readers are invited to join the **Polymath Challenge,** a free seven-day introduction to interdisciplinary learning inspired by this book. Visit the website and social media for new challenges, discussions, and creative tools.

Learning doesn't end with the last page. It begins the moment you decide to see the world through many lenses.

I WANT TO LEARN EVERYTHING:
THE POLYMATH'S PATH

By Gabriel P. Elbert-Rasmussen

About the Author

Gabriel P. Elbert-Rasmussen is an award-winning actor, author, musician, and student of the world around him.

His curiosity spans science, art, philosophy, and craftmanship — disciplines he explores through the lens of everyday refinement and hands-on learning. Whether studying fermentation, practicing etiquette, performing with his friends and family, or experimenting in the kitchen, Gabriel approaches each pursuit with the same goal: to understand how learning itself can become an art form.

I Want to Learn Everything: The Polymath's Path is his first book — the beginning of a broader journey to help others rediscover curiosity, self-mastery, and joy in learning.